Colossians: The Christian's Progress and Preservation

Colossians: The Christian's Progress and Preservation

Andrew de Ville

RITCHIE
CHRISTIAN MEDIA
40 Beansburn, Kilmarnock, Scotland

ISBN 978 1 914273 81 0

COLOSSIANS: THE CHRISTIAN'S PROGRESS
AND PRESERVATION

Printed in Great Britain by Bell & Bain Ltd, Glasgow

Contents

List of Abbreviations

Scripture references throughout the book are taken from
the *Authorised (King James) Version* of the Bible (KJV),
except where indicated by an abbreviation as follows:

ESV - *English Standard Version.*
JND - J N Darby's *New Translation.*
RV - *Revised Version.*

Foreword

In the Preface to each volume in his series *Word Studies in the Greek New Testament*, Professor of Greek Kenneth Samuel Wuest (1893-1961) made two statements that may aptly be quoted here. The first, "This is no book to peruse in one's easy chair. It is designed … for use on the Christian's study table alongside of his Bible", is certainly true of the book you now hold in your hand. The second, "The book is not written for the scholar … it is designed for those who love the Lord and His Word and delight in feasting upon it", applies equally. We do not suggest, of course, that this volume on Colossians cannot be enjoyed as an armchair read, or that is it too light to be profitable to the mature Bible student. Rather, the reader will gain most benefit from a determination to study carefully the author's exposition of the epistle with their Bible open before them.

The twin themes of the believer's progress in understanding truth concerning the Person and work of the Lord Jesus, and the way in which such understanding will preserve them from grievous error, run through the author's exposition of Colossians, particularly the doctrinal chapters. The background to the Gnostic error of the Greeks, and the mysticism of the Jewish false teachers, is not only instructive in the context of the epistle, but it also illustrates the dangers posed today by men who set their own assumed wisdom and knowledge above divine revelation.

Our esteemed brother Andrew has pitched the content of this volume well. He carefully unpacks those verses that, on first reading, can be intimidating, and through careful exposition, explanation and application, he brings the reader to a fuller understanding of the text.

The advice of Professor Wuest should be heeded, for serious Bible study requires a disciplined approach. The reader will thereby benefit most from the many hours of meticulous study that were the genesis of Andrew de Ville's latest book.

Phil Coulson

Author's Preface

Why another book on Colossians? This question faces most authors writing a book on a well-trodden path, and it certainly deserves an answer. The book grew out of a series of 36 expository articles written for *Believer's Magazine*, beginning in the trying days of the COVID-19 pandemic in the Autumn of 2020. The seed had been sown the previous October, when the author had the privilege of speaking at the Culloden assembly's Annual Conference along with brothers Phil Coulson and Alan Gamble. That day, the author had given a message on Colossians chapter 2, and Phil, then the editor of *Believer's Magazine*, suggested that it might be helpful to write some articles on this particular letter. The author duly stored this suggestion for a less busy period! This unexpectedly came in Spring and Summer of 2020, during the first lockdown. Initially, a much shorter set of articles was anticipated but, as it happened, a more detailed study led to more a more detailed set of articles on the Colossian epistle. At various stages, the author was encouraged by the positive comments he received about the series from believers in various parts of the UK, and the enquiry as to whether it was intended to bring the articles together as a book. Hence, another book on Colossians!

A remark about the organisation of this book. Although the main content is largely unchanged from the articles which appeared in *Believer's Magazine*, the organisation of the material is somewhat different. The Contents page indicates how the substance of the epistle has been subdivided; an explanation is found in the Introduction.

I also wish to express my sincere thanks to brother Phil Coulson, without whom this exercise would not have started. His encouragement has been very much appreciated. I am glad to thank Phil, and also Ruth McIlveen, for their hard work in turning my manuscript into a book-ready form. To my daughters Deborah and Joanna, thanks also are due for their diligent checking and proofreading; any remaining errors and typos are, of course, entirely my responsibility.

This book is dedicated to my dear wife Matilda, my daughters Deborah and Joanna, and my sister-in-law Elizabeth. Their love, patience and encouragement are why this book has come to fruition.

Chapter 1

Introduction and Outline

The letter to the Colossians is one of Paul's 'Prison Epistles', written during his first imprisonment in Rome (AD 61-63, Acts 28.30). The letter seems to have been written around AD 61-62, after Paul had been visited by Epaphras (who had been instrumental in preaching the Gospel at Colosse, Col 1.5-8; 4.12), and the subsequent establishment of the Colossian church. From the contents of chapter 4, it appears that the letter was delivered to the Colossians by Tychicus and Onesimus (4.7-9). The inclusion of Onesimus with Tychicus provides a reason for the personal letter Paul also wrote to Philemon. The words of Colossians 2.1 suggest that Paul had not personally been to Colosse. Rather, his knowledge of the Colossian assembly was the result of a report given to him by Epaphras (1.8).

Outline of the Letter

When embarking upon the study of any book of Scripture, it is generally helpful to have an overview of the main contents of the book. This letter is no exception. The epistle follows the general pattern of a Pauline letter: chapters 1 and 2 deal mainly with doctrine; chapters 3 and 4 mainly with the practical applications of this doctrine. Arguably, this is too general to be of much use to the student as it does not begin to address the specific content of the letter. Reading through the letter, one may discern that Paul presents a *triplet of triples*. We will use this internal structure to provide the broad outline set out here and throughout the remainder of this work.

The First Triplet

Chapter 1 contains the first triplet, where three main subjects are addressed:

- Progress at Colosse (1.1-14)
- Pre-eminence of Christ (1.15-22)
- Paul's Service (1.23-29)

The *first element* of this triplet has to do with the theme of *progress*, and this is viewed from two standpoints. In verses 3-8, we see the *progress of the Gospel* which had already been realised at Colosse, and which warranted the expression of thanksgiving by Paul and Timothy (v 3). Then, in verses 9-14, we find the further *progress of the saints* that was still required, and for this Paul and Timothy joined with Epaphras in prayer (4.12). In verse 13, Paul declares that the Father has translated us into the Kingdom of the Son of His love (v 13 margin), and this introduces the *second element* of the first triplet, which focuses on the Person and work of Christ. Again, this section divides into two parts: the first part in verses 15-18, with the interconnecting summary "that in all things he might have the preeminence. For it pleased the Father that in him should all fulness dwell" (vv 18-19), and then the second part in verses 20-22. In verses 15-18, we learn four things the Son of God is: note "who is" (v 15); "he is" (v 17); "he is" (v 18); "who is" (v 18). In verses 20-22, there are four matters which have been accomplished by the death of the Son: peace is made (v 20); the reconciliation of all things (v 20); the reconciliation of believers (v 21); the presentation of believers in God's presence (v 22). The *third element* of the first triplet is devoted to the service of the Apostle Paul. Again, the section from verses 23-29 presents two aspects of Paul's service. The key expression is "am made a minister" (v 23). Paul was a *minister of the Gospel* (v 23) and a *minister of the Church* (v 24). The emphasis here is upon the latter, not because it was more important than his Gospel endeavours, but because he was the vessel through whom the true relationship of the Church and Christ had been disclosed. The key truth here is that Christ is the Head of the Church, and that the Church is His Body. This truth underpins a key part of Paul's argument in chapter 2 (vv 18-19).

The Second Triplet

This triplet covers the content of chapter 2 and the opening four verses of chapter 3, dealing with the theme of the preservation and progress of the saints. The danger facing the Colossians was due to Gnosticism (see later in this Introduction for more detail). This danger contained three main elements, which are treated by Paul in turn:

- Preservation from Philosophy and Deception (2.1-10)
- Preservation from Jewish Ritual and Mysticism (2.11-19)
- Preservation from Asceticism (2.20 - 3.4)

In the *first element*, dealing with philosophy and deception, there are *two warnings*: "this I say, lest any man should beguile you with enticing words" (2.4), and "beware lest any man spoil you" (v 8). In the *second element*, dealing with Jewish ritual and mysticism, there are *two exhortations*: "let no man therefore judge you" (v 16), and "let no man beguile you of your reward" (v 18). In the *third element*, dealing with asceticism, there are *two appeals* to the believer's association with Christ: "if ye be dead with Christ" (v 20), and "if ye then be risen with Christ" (3.1).

The Third Triplet

The third triplet covers the balance of the letter (3.5 - 4.18), and deals with practical matters of Christian character and living, specifically:

- Putting Off and Putting On (3.5-17)
- Personal Relationships (3.18 - 4.6)
- Paul's Friends and Fellow-Servants (4.7-18)

Receiving Christ as Lord and Saviour through faith has profound and far-reaching consequences for each individual believer. The *first element* of this triplet considers behaviours and character traits which need to be "put off" (3.8-9), while there are other behaviours and traits which need to be "put on" (vv 10-13). This amounts to "[putting] off the old man with his deeds" (v 9) and "[putting] on the new" (v 10). More detailed discussion of the section will be dealt with later in this book. Furthermore, the Christian does not live an isolated life. The character virtues outlined in verses 5-17 are to be seen in the context of relationships: family relationships, social relationships, and relationships generally with "them that are without" (4.5), evidently referring to unbelievers. This is the subject matter of the *second element* of the triplet covered in 3.18 - 4.6. Finally, in the *third element* (4.7-18), Paul returns to his personal circumstances, and names, with comments, his companions in service, along with concluding instructions to the assembly in Colosse.

The above outline has been adopted to provide the structure for the discussion of the main substance of this epistle. It is acknowledged that this involves a slight departure from the usual practise in commentaries of rigidly following the chapter structure of a letter.

Ephesians and Colossians: Parallel Epistles

The reader of the New Testament will be aware that certain letters can be paired together. This pairing arises in one of two ways. There are the obvious first and second epistles written to either a specified church (for example, 1 and 2 Corinthians; 1 and 2 Thessalonians), to a specified individual (1 and 2 Timothy), or by a specified author (1 and 2 Peter; 1, 2 and 3 John). There is a second way in which epistles are paralleled: that is, the same basic content is covered in both. It is easy to see that Romans and Galatians stand together, and so too Ephesians stands with Colossians. This parallel may be taken further. What Galatians is to Romans, Colossians is to Ephesians. In Romans, we find an *exposition* of the truth of the Gospel; in Galatians, a *defence* of the truth of the Gospel. In Ephesians, Paul *expounds* the mystery of Christ and the Church – the Church being the Body of Christ; in Colossians, he *defends* this same truth against false teaching which would, in effect, deny this revelation.

However, there are a number of contrasts between Ephesians and

Colossians which are helpful to observe. We note two. In Ephesians, the focus is upon the Body of Christ, comprising believing Jew and Gentile, with former distinctions removed (Eph 2). In Colossians, while the Body of Christ is found, the focus is on Christ as the Head of the Body. The reason is that, in Colossians, the error which Paul is seeking to combat is a direct satanic assault on the doctrine of the Person and work of Christ. Secondly, in Ephesians, there is extensive reference to the Person and ministry of the Holy Spirit. In Colossians, there is one direct reference to the Holy Spirit (1.8), the focus being upon the pre-eminence and sufficiency of Christ as the Head of the Church.

The Nature of the Colossian Peril

One issue of immediate interest is to identify the nature of the danger to which the Colossians were exposed, and which was of real concern to Paul (2.1). At present, it suffices to note that the grave danger posed to the Colossians was from so-called Gnostics. Gnosticism (from the Greek word *gnosis*, meaning knowledge) is by no means simple to understand. It involved the synthesis of three main elements: Greek philosophy, Jewish ordinances and mysticism, and Eastern asceticism. Adherents to Gnosticism made pretentious claims to higher knowledge and insight, which turned out to be merely vain speculations. The danger for the Colossian believers was the attempt to incorporate Christianity within the Gnostic framework, and to thereby diminish the glory and sufficiency of Christ. This danger persisted, and continued to develop, to the end of the apostolic age and beyond. The Apostle John had the same error in view in his epistles (see Postscript) and, in his Gospel, provided historical evidence to refute the claims of Gnostic false teachers.

It is worth noting Paul's approach to dealing with this error. Firstly, he positively presents the doctrine of Christ and promotes the truth of His pre-eminence; this makes the epistle a joy to the believer's heart, even if we do not grasp the precise nature of the Gnostic threat. Secondly, he divides the error into its component elements, and deals with each in turn (the reader will find this approach taken by Paul in chapter 2). Paul's method, inspired of course by the Holy Spirit, is well worth following today. The positive presentation of the truth of God and, in particular, the doctrine of Christ, both regarding His Person and work, is our greatest preservation against error. This requires more than mere sound bites; it demands the precise, contextual exposition of the Scriptures in the power of the Holy Spirit. Even within the confines of this letter, we will find an extensive presentation of the Person and work of our Lord Jesus Christ. Secondly, when dealing with error, it is often helpful to break it into its key components, and then to refute each in turn. The pattern provided for us by the Holy Spirit, through Paul, is one we would do well to follow.

The Church at Colosse

At the time of writing, it is clear from Colossians 4.12 that Epaphras had come from Colosse and was with Paul in Rome. In his letter to Philemon, Paul names Epaphras, and designates him "my fellowprisoner" (v 23). From Colossians 1.7, it is clear that Epaphras had played a significant part in preaching the Gospel in Colosse. There was evidently fruit in salvation, and an assembly was established which probably met in the house of Philemon (Phm 2). The emergence of the Gnostic threat led Epaphras to seek Paul in Rome, and there he informed the apostle of the work of God in Colosse. Paul's counsel to the assembly is the content of the Colossian epistle. It is likely that the epistle was carried to Colosse by Tychicus (Col 4.7), who was accompanied by Onesimus (v 9). Onesimus was certainly known by Philemon, having been his slave; it seems that he had deserted Philemon's household, eventually making his way to Rome. There he came into contact with Paul, and was converted to Christ. The Epistle to Philemon was probably written and taken to Colosse at the same time, to deal with the potential difficulty of how Philemon would react to the arrival of his formerly unfaithful slave, who was now "a brother … in the Lord" (Phm 16).

Chapter 2

Progress at Colosse (1.1-14)

The opening section of the letter consists of three readily discernible sections:

- Paul's Greeting (1.1-2)
- Paul's Thanksgiving: Progress of the Gospel (1.3-8)
- Paul's Prayer: Progress of the Saints (1.9-14)

Paul's Greeting (1.1-2)

Paul, an apostle of Jesus Christ by the will of God, and Timotheus our brother, to the saints and faithful brethren in Christ which are at Colosse: Grace be unto you, and peace, from God our Father and the Lord Jesus Christ.

As in all Paul's letters, it is wise not to rush past the introduction, overlooking the greeting to press on to what one might regard as the main business. It is well to carefully weigh the opening words. Four matters are presented in verses 1 and 2:

1. The Writer (1.1)
2. The Companion (1.1)
3. The Recipients (1.2)
4. The Greeting (1.2)

There is no doubt about the identity of the author: "Paul, an apostle of Jesus Christ by the will of God" (v 1). Paul asserts his authority as an apostle of Christ Jesus (RV); it is as such that he will write authoritatively on the subject of the Lord Jesus Christ, and press upon the Colossians the claims that this exalted Man in Heaven has upon them. In view of the dangerous error faced by the Colossian saints, the reference to Paul's apostleship stresses his right to both expose the nature of the error and to present the truth, particularly as this relates to the Person, work and present ministry of Christ. Secondly, Paul was confident that his apostleship was through the will of God. Paul did not choose to be an apostle; it was God's will for his life of service for the Lord. May we all arrive at the same settled understanding of the will of God in the matter of our own service for the Lord. Later, Paul would desire for the Colossians that they "be filled with the knowledge of his will" (v 9).

Next, Paul is careful to identify his companion: "Timotheus our brother" (v 1). This expression describes a family relationship, and Paul speaks of Timothy in terms of equality; Timothy and Paul were brothers in the Lord. This speaks volumes about how Paul valued and regarded Timothy. While it was true that Paul was a 'sent-one' of Christ Jesus and, as such, had a unique ministry, he nonetheless valued the fellowship and ministry of Timothy. We do well to embrace the way in which Paul regarded his fellow-servants in our relationships with our brethren and sisters in the Lord. No matter the gift we have, no matter the prominence we may have among the saints, we need the fellowship and ministry of other believers.

Verse 2 identifies the recipients of the letter: "to the saints and faithful brethren in Christ which are at Colosse". In this expression, Paul is not addressing two different groups of people, one called saints another called faithful brethren; rather, he gives a two-fold description of the believers at Colosse. As saints, they were God's holy ones; here is the great dignity of the believer in the Lord Jesus - we are saints by divine calling (1 Cor 1.2). Much of Christendom is seriously mistaken about the term 'saints'; in the New Testament, it is a term used of every believer in their relationship with God. Of course, we must now live up to this designation by leading lives which are set apart to God, and set apart from the world and the evil which permeates it. It is a term which captures God's intention for each of us, that we be "holy" (Col 1.22). If "saints" describes what God has made us, the second description, "faithful brethren", views us from the standpoint of human responsibility. The same Colossians were "faithful" in their Christian testimony; they were proving to be trustworthy in their handling of, and engagement with, divine things. While it is true that Paul was concerned for the Colossians in view of Gnostic error, they were nevertheless marked at this point by faithfulness to the Lord. Paul is burdened in this epistle to ensure that this continues, so that they are not derailed by the spoiling influence of false teachers and false doctrine. The Colossians were "brethren", stressing their relationship with each other within the family of God. Their faithfulness was seen in their dealings with each other, as well as their fidelity to the Lord. May we all live up to this two-fold description of the believers: saints and faithful brethren. None of us can be complacent: past faithfulness is simply not enough; present preservation is required. It is well to note at this juncture that the epistle, while addressed to the saints at Colosse, was also for the benefit of the church at Laodicea (4.16); similarly, the letter received by the Laodiceans was to be read to the Colossians.

We arrive finally at the actual greeting: "Grace be unto you, and peace, from God our Father and the Lord Jesus Christ" (1.2). They had been the recipients of the grace of God in receiving salvation, but here Paul desires that they continue to know the grace which flows from "God our Father". This assumes the enjoyment of our relationship with God as Father, knowing that we are His sons and children. Along with grace (His unmerited favour) comes peace; the activity of the false teachers had brought uncertainty and disquiet, potentially unsettling the saints. From God our Father comes peace. This "grace ... and peace" is viewed as coming from both "God our Father and the Lord Jesus Christ" and, as such, implies the equality of the Father and the Son. The full title "Lord Jesus Christ" impresses us with the majesty of His Person; His supreme authority and deity (Lord), His perfect humanity (Jesus), His Messiahship (Christ). Paul commences the letter by directing the Colossians, and us, to God our Father and the Lord Jesus Christ; this is always a good exercise, to turn from men and their wisdom and to focus on God, our relationship with Him, and the greatness of our Lord and Saviour. This greeting reminds us that the resources required for both individual and corporate testimony come from the bountiful supply of our Father and our Lord Jesus Christ. The Godhead desires us to rely on divine grace, and to experience, on an ongoing basis, divine peace.

Paul's Thanksgiving: Progress of the Gospel (1.3-8)

> We give thanks to God and the Father of our Lord Jesus Christ, praying always for you, since we heard of your faith in Christ Jesus, and of the love which ye have to all the saints, for the hope which is laid up for you in heaven, whereof ye heard before in the word of the truth of the gospel; which is come unto you, as it is in all the world; and bringeth forth fruit, as it doth also in you, since the day ye heard of it, and knew the grace of God in truth: as ye also learned of Epaphras our dear fellowservant, who is for you a faithful minister of Christ; who also declared unto us your love in the Spirit.

We now focus on Paul's account of the progress of the Gospel at Colosse (vv 3-8). Although it seems that Paul had not personally visited Colosse (2.1), he demonstrates a deep care for the welfare and progress of the believers there. The shepherd heart of the apostle shines through.

In this section, the following matters are addressed:

- Paul's Thanksgiving (1.3)
- The Impact of the Gospel (note the references to faith, love and hope) (1.4-5)
- The Description of the Gospel (1.5)
- The Scope of the Gospel (1.6)
- The Fruitfulness of the Gospel (1.6)
- The Messenger who Taught the Gospel (1.7-8)

The section begins with Paul and Timothy's thanksgiving: "We give thanks to God and the Father of our Lord Jesus Christ, praying always for you" (v 3). A common feature in Paul's writing is his oft reference to prayer and thanksgiving. Here is no exception. Paul felt a deep sense of gratitude to God for the salvation of these Colossians. It did not matter that he was not instrumental in their conversion; he was grateful for hearing such news, and he continued in prayer for them. The detailed content of his prayer awaits in verses 9-14. It is instructive to observe the description of the Person to whom this thanksgiving is directed: "the God and Father of our Lord Jesus Christ" (JND). In verse 2, the focus is on our relationship with the Father; grace and peace come from "God our Father". Here, the focus is upon the relationship between divine Persons: as the God of our Lord Jesus Christ, we view God's relationship with the Man Christ Jesus; as the Father of our Lord Jesus Christ, we view the Father's relationship with "his dear Son" (v 13) (or, as in the *Revised Version*, "Son of his love"). In the salvation of these Colossians, Paul sees with gratitude the results of the Calvary-work of the Lord Jesus in the redemption and reconciliation to God of these precious souls. On a practical note, thanksgiving and prayer are to be directed to God the Father, in the Name of the Son and in the power of the Holy Spirit (Jn 16.23-26; Eph 2.18; 6.18).

Verse 4 summarises the impact of the Gospel on the Colossians: Paul makes reference to their "faith in Christ Jesus, and ... love which ye have to all the saints". We can see that faith is Godward, and love here is manward. Their faith was in an exalted Man in Heaven; He was now their trust, and their confidence was in Him alone. In chapter 2 verse 5, he also commends the "stedfastness of your faith in Christ". There was a change in their attitude towards God's people; they exhibited love to all the saints. Before conversion, they had been "enemies in [their] mind by wicked works" (1.21), but they had now been reconciled to God, one evidence of which was a change of heart to those who belonged to God, His saints. They now loved "all the saints" (v 4). We should expect in those that profess the Name of Christ these two evidences of reality: faith in Christ Jesus and love for the saints. There are two practical observations to be made. Firstly, it is helpful that we view our fellow-believers as saints, to see to each other in terms of what we are to God. This should help us love our fellow-believers as we ought. Secondly, there is a practical difficulty when our fellow-believers do not act in a saintly way in our eyes. What then? Paul addresses this later when he exhorts us to be "longsuffering; forbearing one another, and forgiving one another" (3.12-13). The flaws in the conduct of fellow-believers toward us must not be used as justification for not loving them.

Having noted their faith and love in verse 4, we are not surprised to read about hope in verse 5: "for the hope which is laid up for you in heaven". We cite the rendering of two other versions to amplify Paul's teaching here: "because of the hope which is laid up for you in the heavens" (RV); "on account of the hope which is laid up for you in the heavens" (JND).

Both the *Revised Version* and J N Darby's reading make clear that we are to regard the hope as the reason for what has proceeded. There is, then, a question as to whether verse 5 links back to verse 3, providing the reason why Paul was giving thanks for them; he had in view their glorious future "in the heavens", and this prompted thanksgiving. Alternatively, verse 5 may connect to the last statement of verse 4, providing us with an insight as to why they loved all the saints. They had in view the future of the saints "in the heavens", and their certain future prospect was motivation for loving all saints in the present. This is helpful practically, for considering what our fellow-believers will be in the future should help us love them in the present. The observant reader will note that both the *Revised Version* and J N Darby highlight that 'heaven' is a plural term – "the heavens". What did Paul particularly have in mind? Note, too, that "laid up" is translated "appointed" in Hebrews 9.27, and observe the expression in Colossians 1.27: "the hope of glory". We learn more of this in Colossians 3.4: "When Christ, who is our life, shall appear, then shall ye also appear with him in glory". Putting this together, we see that the Colossians had (and all believers of this Church age have) a hope to which we are appointed in the heavens, which will be realised when we are manifest with Christ in glory, at His appearing. This will remain so throughout the duration of the Millennial reign of Christ, when the home of the saints will be the "great city, the holy Jerusalem, descending out of heaven from God, having the glory of God" (Rev 21.10-11). Peter expresses a similar truth in 1 Peter 1.4, where we read of "an inheritance incorruptible, and undefiled, and that fadeth not away, reserved in heaven [the heavens] for you".

The nature of this hope was not new to them - they had "heard before in the word of the truth of the gospel" (Col 1.5). The description of the message is striking and unique. Paul could simply have written that they had heard the Gospel, which was true. But, rather, he stresses that they had heard "the truth of the gospel". The message they heard was the truth and no fable. They were right to believe it! Perhaps Paul has in mind the unsettling impact of the false teachers to whom the Colossians were exposed, and so stresses that what they had heard was truth. The expression also includes the particular Gospel truths they heard, such as redemption, forgiveness and reconciliation, to mention but three we find in verses 14 and 21. These certainly form part of the truth of the Gospel, which men need to hear. Finally, he notes that they heard the "word of the truth of the gospel". Amazingly, the truth of the Gospel is conveyed by words, spoken or written. As we have noted, in this very letter, Paul identifies some of the words used to convey the truth (with explanations, of course); we should use these words in our day too!

The scope of the message is captured by the words, "which is come unto you, as it is in all the world" (v 6). These words contain the germ of an important principle: the message of the Gospel came to the Colossians. During the Millennial Kingdom, men will seek God at Jerusalem (see, for example, Isaiah 2.2-4) but, in Colosse, God sought men in their own city. The experience of the Ethiopian eunuch (Acts 8.26-40) illustrates the point; he came to Jerusalem to worship, yet did not find the Gospel there (which is perhaps surprising), but God found him on his return journey when the Gospel came to him through Philip.

The Gospel was fruitful: "and bringeth forth fruit, as it doth also in you, since the day ye heard of it, and knew the grace of God in truth" (Col 1.6). There is a sense in which the believers were themselves the fruit of the Gospel; in another sense, the message had brought about a change in their lives, so there was fruit in them. This is the focus here in the words "in you"; the faith and love we have noted being included in this fruit.

Finally, we learn of the messenger who proclaimed the Gospel (vv 7-8). The description of Epaphras is touching; he was a beloved fellow-servant in Paul's eyes, and was in the same business as the apostle. He was also "a faithful minister of Christ" (v 7). Two words for 'servant' are used by Paul. Firstly, Epaphras was a fellow-bondslave, stressing that he was the possession of another, namely, the Lord. Secondly, he was a faithful 'deacon' of Christ. Here, the focus is on the substance of his ministry: he faithfully brought Christ to the Colossians. As such, Epaphras is a valuable pattern for every servant of the Lord. We, too, need to be faithful, and bring Christ both to the saints and the unsaved. In chapter 4 verse 12, we learn of another valuable aspect of Epaphras' service - his labour in prayer for the Colossian saints.

Verse 8 confirms that Paul had learned of the state of the Colossian saints from the lips of Epaphras. Specifically, he had declared to Paul and Timothy the love of the believers. The expression, "your love in the Spirit", seems to suggest that the love of the Colossian saints, whether Godward or saintward, was the result of the working of the Holy Spirit. The Holy Spirit had both prompted and empowered the exercise of their love. This love was not simply in verbal expressions, but also in practical demonstrations, the details of which are given in chapters 3 and 4. The term "the Spirit" is to be understood as referring to the Holy Spirit and is, therefore, the only direct reference to the Holy Spirit in the whole epistle.

Paul's Prayer: Progress of the Saints (1.9-14)

> For this cause we also, since the day we heard it, do not cease to pray for you, and to desire that ye might be filled with the knowledge of his will in all wisdom and spiritual understanding; that ye might walk worthy of the Lord unto all pleasing, being fruitful in every good work, and increasing in the knowledge of God; strengthened with all might, according to his glorious power, unto all patience and longsuffering with joyfulness; giving thanks unto the Father, which hath made us meet to be partakers of the inheritance of the saints in light: who hath delivered us from the power of darkness, and hath translated us into the kingdom of his dear Son: in whom we have redemption through His blood, even the forgiveness of sins.

Having heard from Epaphras of the salvation of the Colossian saints (1.3-8), Paul desired to see them progress. In verses 9-14, we have his detailed prayer with this in mind. He makes seven particular requests for them, desiring that they might:

1. Know the will of God (1.9)
2. "Walk worthy of the Lord" (1.10)
3. "[Be] fruitful in every good work" (1.10)
4. "[Increase] in the knowledge of God" (1.10)
5. Be strengthened (1.11)
6. Be patient and longsuffering (1.11)
7. "[Give] thanks unto the Father" (1.12-14)

These are evidently weighty matters, and Paul's prayer provides a pattern for every praying saint who has the spiritual progress of fellow-believers at heart.

Verse 9 introduces Paul's prayer with the words, "for this cause we also, since the day we heard it, do not cease to pray for you". The evidence of their faith and love demonstrated to Paul the reality of their conversion, and he now devoted himself to pray for them. Note the words "we also"; Paul and Timothy had now joined with Epaphras (4.12) in a sustained exercise of prayer for the Colossian believers. This is a challenging example to follow - maintaining a prayerful interest in the welfare and progress of the saints. We will now look at Paul's seven prayerful requests in more detail:

1. Know the will of God (1.9)

The first matter in his prayer has to do with the will of God: Paul desires "that ye might be filled with the knowledge of his will in all wisdom and spiritual understanding" (v 9). This expression is rich with important teaching, which we will now explore at some length. The first point is that, for saints, the will of God is important. Paul has already made reference to this in relation to his own apostleship (v 1), and will later refer to another aspect in verse 27, relating to God's desire for us to appreciate the relationship the Church has with Christ, and its glorious future. Next, note that whatever is involved in the will of God here, it can be known. Indeed, the idea in the word "knowledge" is full knowledge. Full knowledge is not to be mistaken for exhaustive knowledge; we can have an extensive knowledge of a subject without it being exhaustive. There is an obvious question we must now address:

how can the will of God be known? For the Colossians, as for us, this very letter provides a full knowledge of the will of God. While there may be particular questions which arise in life - Who should I marry? Should I take this job? Where should I live? - this letter contains an extensive description of what God wills for us and requires of us. This relates both to the present and the future, both personally and collectively. For example, in chapter 3, we are left in no doubt about the kind of people God wills us to be.

The knowledge of His will should be accompanied with "wisdom and spiritual understanding". For the Greek, the idea of wisdom was the mental excellency in its highest and fullest sense,[1] whereas the common use in the Old Testament is that of the practical good sense in applying the will of God in the situations of life. It involves having an insight into the true nature of things,[2] and the practical sense in application. It is knowing and carrying out the right course of action in each situation. This is Paul's meaning when, later, he exhorts that we "walk in wisdom toward them that are without" (4.5).

Understanding involves putting information together, drawing appropriate conclusions, and seeing relationships.[3] Perhaps an illustration may help. Consider a jigsaw puzzle: the individual pieces are like bits of information or knowledge; putting the pieces together so that we see the connections between pieces and the overall picture is like developing our understanding. There is another point of practical importance: it is quicker to gain knowledge than to acquire understanding. Paul's advice to Timothy in 2 Timothy 2.7 is apposite: "Consider what I say; and the Lord give thee understanding in all things". It takes time to "consider" the word of God but, ultimately, in prayerful exercise, the Lord does give understanding. There is a second point: there are degrees of understanding, and with increasing consideration our understanding will deepen. This is important for younger believers to grasp - instant understanding in spiritual matters simply does not happen! The use of the word "spiritual" qualifies the nature of the things Paul desires them to understand; they are things relating to the spiritual rather than the physical realm. The important point is this: the Colossians could acquire a full knowledge of the will of God, and have wisdom and understanding, without recourse to Gnostic speculations. Indeed, Gnostic speculations could never lead to knowing the will of God. A further point is vital to stress: the will of God is never contrary to the revelation of His will in Scripture. To claim to be doing the will of God on a course which contradicts, or is outside the revelation of, Scripture is a deception – it is, rather, the expression of our own will or the will of men.

2. "Walk worthy of the Lord" (1.10)

Paul's second request demonstrates that knowledge of the will of God must be translated into practice: "that ye might walk worthy of the Lord unto all pleasing" (v 10). Here, the word "walk" carries the thought of walking about: it refers to the activity of life. Carrying out the will of God, even as defined in this letter, will result in a manner of life which is worthy of the Lord; a life which is befitting the Lord and is pleasing to Him. Living in the good of this request has the positive benefit of turning our eyes away from ourselves to the Lord. When tempted to justify a course of action on the grounds that there is no harm in it, we can look to the Lord and reflect on whether the action is worthy of Him and pleasing to Him. He then becomes the measure or standard we use in making decisions. Perhaps if we had this truth before us more, we would spare ourselves from the inconsistency to which some of us are prone.

3. "[Be] fruitful in every good work" (1.10)

Paul desires that the Colossians be fruitful in their lives for the Lord: "being fruitful in every good work" (v 10). At this juncture, Paul is not specific about the works he has in mind, save that they are "good", in the sense of being beneficial in character. Specific examples may be found in chapters 3 and 4. The bearing of fruit is not to be viewed as a one-off event, but is to be a continuous feature of the life of the saint. Furthermore, the fruit is not simply good works; it is what is produced in the life of the believer by engaging in doing good. For example, we are to put on kindness, which involves meeting the need of others (3.12). Hence, by so doing, the fruit of kindness becomes evident in our lives. Whilst the practical work of kindness meets a particular need, it is the kindness which motivated that work which is the fruit that Paul desires. That said, the only way to show kindness is by practical activity. The question is, then, for whom is this fruit? The Lord Himself explained that it is the Father who is looking for "fruit", "more fruit" and "much fruit" (Jn 15.2, 8).

4. "[Increase] in the knowledge of God" (1.10)

The first apostolic request focused on the will of God; now Paul desires that they be "increasing in the knowledge of God" (v 10). The first request has to do with knowing what God wills; now it is knowledge of God Himself. The thrilling implication of Paul's request is that a 'full knowledge' of God is possible for each believer, recognising that *full* knowledge is not *exhaustive* knowledge. Even restricting attention to this letter alone, there is certainly a full revelation of God for us to enjoy. Surely this is the essence of eternal life as explained by the Son of God: "this is life eternal, that they might know thee the only true God, and Jesus Christ, whom thou hast sent" (Jn 17.3). For us, this increasing knowledge comes through the One who is the "image of the invisible God" (Col 1.15), namely, our Lord Jesus Christ, in whom "dwelleth all the fulness of the Godhead bodily" (2.9). The Gnostic had nothing of this quality to offer! Before concluding, there is a grammatical point worth considering. J N Darby renders the expression under consideration as "growing by the true knowledge of God". That is, the knowledge of God is the instrument for growth in the believer. There is merit in this thought. After all, later, John would write of the fathers in the family of God, "I write unto you, fathers, because ye have known him that is from the beginning" (1 Jn 2.13). John associates spiritual maturity here with knowing the Son of God.

5. Be strengthened (1.11)

Verse 11 gives the full form of this request: "Strengthened with all might, according to his glorious power, unto all patience and longsuffering with joyfulness". Both J N Darby and the *Revised Version* render verse 11 as "strengthened with all power, according to the might of his glory". Though it is true that the power of God is indeed glorious, the more accurate reading is "the might of his glory", and it requires some explanation. Before dealing with this, let us note some basic truths. The

Colossian believers, as with us, required ongoing strengthening. The need for this is explained in the context: strengthening is required both to "walk worthy of the Lord" and to show "all patience and longsuffering with joyfulness" (v 10). Who is the source of this strength? In Ephesians 3.16, Paul prays that the believer might be "strengthened with might by his Spirit in the inner man", while, in Philippians 4.13, the apostle acknowledges, "I can do all things through Christ which strengtheneth me". Thus, the strength comes from God. Here the focus is rather different: the believer is to be strengthened "with all power". This is an incredible statement; "all power" is the resource available to the saint. Clearly, only God possesses all power, so there is no inconsistency with the Scriptures cited, but the emphasis here is on the inexhaustible supply. Each saint, through the course of life, can be strengthened from the unlimited, undiminished supply of "all power".

Next, this power is in keeping with the "might of his glory". Note that this expression links together God's might and God's glory. There are occasions when this was seen in the Lord's earthly ministry: recall, "this beginning of miracles did Jesus in Cana of Galilee, and manifested forth his glory" (Jn 2.11). The display of the Lord's power in turning water to wine thus expressed the glory of His Person. Similarly, in the raising of Lazarus from the dead, the Son of God displayed His unique glory in a work of power (11.4, 40). In the present context, this connection is viewed from a different perspective: in appreciating the glory of God (and, surely, as we increase in our knowledge of God, this will be the case) there is spiritual strengthening for the saint. This principle was illustrated when "the God of glory appeared unto ... Abraham" (Acts 7.2); the result was that Abraham was so enabled to leave the religious confusion of Ur. At the end of the chapter, Stephen saw the glory of God, and was able endure his trial to the end (v 55). There is enabling power in appreciating the glory of God.

6. Be patient and longsuffering (1.11)

This connects with the intention of the apostle here; he understood that the Colossians would be required to show "patience" (that is, endurance) and "longsuffering" (that is, showing self-restraint when provoked). In the challenges we encounter in our spiritual life, possibly as here, resisting false teachers and their false teaching, we need to show endurance and longsuffering. It is important to recognise that we are presently in a sphere of spiritual conflict in which the Evil One is active in contesting "the faith": as Jude exhorts, "earnestly contend for the faith" (Jude v 3). In this, we need divine strengthening to continue in a worthy walk for the Lord.

Remarkably, Paul adds, "with joyfulness" (Col 1.11). This seems at odds with the circumstances which require the exercise of patience and longsuffering. How can we then have joyfulness? As usual, the context supplies the answer. Surely, there is fulness of joy as we increase in the knowledge of God (v 10). After all, "we also joy in God" (Rom 5.11), and "rejoice in the Lord" (Phil 3.1). It may be that we cannot rejoice in our circumstances, but we can find our joy in God. We can also find joy in appreciating what God has done for us; this leads us into verses 12-14. Furthermore, there is joy in appreciating the glory of the Lord Jesus Christ, as we find thrillingly presented in verses 14-22, and joy in our relationship with both the Father and the Son. There is also joy in our relationship with our fellow-saints, and joy in our service for the Lord.

7. "[Give] thanks unto the Father" (1.12-14)

In verse 3, Paul and Timothy gave thanks for the salvation of the Colossian saints; here, Paul wants the Colossian saints to give thanks to the Father for what He has done for them, and for what they have in Christ. There are four particular matters to prompt thanksgiving:

i. "Made … meet [for] the inheritance of the saints in light" (1.12)
ii. "Delivered from the power [authority] of darkness" (1.13)
iii. "Translated … into the kingdom of his dear Son" (1.13)
iv. "In whom we have redemption through his blood, even the forgiveness of sins" (1.14)

i. "Made ... meet [for] the inheritance of the saints in light" (1.12): The Father has endued us with a fitness such that we can share in the portion of the saints in the light. This is the proper position of the saints before God. The Colossians were no longer in spiritual darkness, but now had the place of saints before God, who "is light" (1 Jn 1.5). There is an important parallel to observe: the God who is Light will have before Him "saints in light"; the God who is Love (1 Jn 4.8) has chosen us to be "before him in love" (Eph 1.4). The import is this: God fits us to be in His presence and intends that we appreciate what He is essentially - light and love. While there will be a particular fulfilment of this when we are in Heaven, it is spiritually true now of every believer; we are saints in light.

ii. "Delivered from the power [authority] of darkness" (1.13): Before the Colossians believed the Gospel, they were under the authority of darkness. This darkness was spiritual and moral, and they needed divine deliverance from the authority it exercised over them; this the Father has done. Elsewhere, Paul stresses the gravity of this condition: "ye were once darkness, but are now light in the Lord" (Eph 5.8, RV). They could not emancipate themselves; they required a deliverer. The "power [authority] of darkness" (Col 1.13) stands here for Satan and his hosts, who are active in keeping men in a state of darkness. There is a similar thought in Ephesians 6.12: "the rulers of the darkness of this world". From this darkness the Father has rescued us; we now know the Father and the Son, which is surely ample reason for giving thanks.

iii. "Translated ... into the kingdom of his dear Son" (1.13): The position of the believer is seen to have changed. Having taken us from the domain where darkness holds sway, the Father has introduced us into a new realm: "the kingdom of his dear Son". While there is undoubtedly a future aspect of the Kingdom, this Scripture implies that we are already subjects in the Son's Kingdom. This is the realm where He is sovereign and where His authority is acknowledged. The description of the Son is most precious. Again, it is well worth noting that the reading in J N Darby's *New Translation* and the *Revised Version* is "the Son of his love". This, then, is a realm where the Father's love for His Son is appreciated, and the Son is known as the object of His Father's love. While we rejoice that the Father loves us (1 Jn 3.1), it is precious to also be able to appreciate the Father's love for His Son. This is a place of nearness to God where we are able, in measure, to enter and share the feelings of His heart for His Son. This again highlights the poverty of the Gnostic position, which posited a huge gulf between God and man. By way of contrast, through the Gospel, we have been brought into a relationship in which we can begin to appreciate the love between the Persons of the Godhead. Again, this is surely a cause for expressions of thanksgivings.

iv. "In whom we have redemption through his blood, even the forgiveness of sins" (1.14): Our thankfulness is not only in view of what the Father has done, but also in light of what we have in spiritual union with Christ. In this union, we have redemption, the forgiveness of sins. Redemption is a release effected upon the payment of a ransom price. The ransom price is "his blood"; the release is here "the forgiveness of sins". What cause for thanksgiving is this! In view of the shed blood of the Son at Calvary, paying in full the required price for redemption, we have the forgiveness of sins. This is not only a great relief for the soul, but an ongoing reason to express our thanksgiving to the Father.

Chapter 3

Pre-eminence of Christ (1.15-22)

Having introduced the Son of the Father's love in verse 13 of chapter 1, Paul now expounds the delightful and necessary theme of the pre-eminence of the Son. This positive presentation of the glory of the Son was both an education to the saints at Colosse and, at the same time, a preservation from the pernicious error they faced. The same remains true. The best way to preserve the saints is by the positive presentation of the truth, and notably the doctrine of Christ. Before proceeding, we note the text before us:

> Who is the image of the invisible God, the firstborn of every creature: for by him were all things created, that are in heaven, and that are in earth, visible and invisible, whether they be thrones, or dominions, or principalities, or powers: all things were created by him, and for him: and he is before all things, and by him all things consist. And he is the head of the body, the church: who is the beginning, the firstborn from the dead; that in all things He might have the preeminence. For it pleased the Father that in him should all fulness dwell; and, having made peace through the blood of his cross, by him to reconcile all things unto himself; by him, I say, whether they be things in earth, or things in heaven. And you, that were sometime alienated and enemies in your mind by wicked works, yet now hath he reconciled in the body of his flesh through death, to present you holy and unblameable and unreproveable in his sight (Col 1.15-22).

The above verses are probably the best-known verses in the whole letter. The words of verse 18, "that in all things he might have the preeminence", are an apt summary of the teaching of the apostle here.

The Lord is seen to be pre-eminent in relation to:

- *The Revelation of God (1.15)* – He is the image of the invisible God
- *All Creation (1.16-17)* – He is the Firstborn, because He is the Creator
- *The Church (1.18)* – He is the Head
- *Resurrection (1.18)* – He is the Beginning and Firstborn
- *Reconciliation (1.19-22)* – Peace has been made through His death

The Revelation of God (1.15) – He is the image of the invisible God

The Scripture states, "Who is the image of the invisible God". The word "who" connects with the previous verses, where we have learned about "the Son of his love" (v 13, RV). Thus, it is the Son of the Father's love who is the image of the invisible God. Next, we need to consider the word "image". In Greek thought, an image shares in reality what it represents.[4] Here, the Son is the perfect representation and manifestation of the invisible God. This is the case, "for in him dwelleth all the fulness of the Godhead bodily" (2.9). Elsewhere, the same truth is presented: "who being the brightness of his glory, and the express image of his person" (Heb 1.3); "who is the image of God" (2 Cor 4.4). In Hebrews 1.3, the words quoted declare that the Son is the exact expression of God's substance. Though God is spirit (Jn 4.24), He still has substance, referring to His essential Being. This essence belongs also in entirety to the Son, and is the reason why He is the brightness of the glory of God. This is not reflected glory; rather, it is the essential glory of deity emanating from the Son who is in every sense God. Here, God is said to be "invisible", that is, not seen. In effect, the Son has made the invisible God visible. Though God remains invisible, He is not unknowable! We can get to know Him through the Son, who is the perfect and complete representation of all that God is, Himself being God.

Although this statement stands majestic and true in isolation, it perfectly fits the context of Paul's prayer (Col 1.9-14), in which he requested for the Colossians that they increase in the knowledge of

God. Was this a reasonable request? Was it attainable? We must give a resounding 'Yes' to both questions; but only because the Son of God is the image of the unseen God. Readers will have in mind relevant Scriptures from John's Gospel in this connection: "No man has seen God at any time; the only begotten Son, which is in the bosom of the Father, he hath declared him" (Jn 1.18); "If ye had known me, ye should have known my Father also" (14.7).

Thus, the Son has declared God the Father (indeed, He has declared God *as* Father), so that those who know the Son also know the Father, by reason of the essential equality of Father and Son. Still considering the context of verse 15, we might wonder how this connects to what follows in verses 16-17. The key question is: in what sphere is the invisible God made known? The answer is the sphere of creation. God has revealed Himself in His creation by His Son. The relationship of the Son to creation is now developed by the apostle.

All Creation (1.16-17) – He is the Firstborn, because He is the Creator

The Son stands in relation to creation as the Firstborn; He is "firstborn of every creature" (v 15). Both the *Revised Version* and J N Darby give the reading, "firstborn of all creation". This is preferable, as the creatorial work of the Son extends not only to creatures (namely, living beings) but also to inanimate creation, including the heavens and the earth. The statement here is both extensive and exhaustive: "all creation" embraces all created things. As John writes, "All things received being through him, and without him not one thing received being which has received being" (Jn 1.3, JND). These words are exceptionally important. John identifies a category to which we might attach the label, 'things which have received being', and claims that each thing in this category owes its existence to the Son (as the Eternal Word). That is, all that has come into being - all creation - came into being through the Son. One immediate implication is that the Son Himself *cannot* therefore belong to this category of created things! The Creator of all things was not, and indeed could not, be created, otherwise, the claim of John 1.3 is contradicted. As many readers are aware, there are those who blasphemously infer from the word "firstborn" that the Son is a created being, but this is a misunderstanding of the word "firstborn". As T Bentley[5] aptly notes, "Paul's language in this and the verses following nullifies such a notion. He uses *prōtotokos* ("firstborn"), not *prōtoktistos* ('first created')". The word denotes rank, priority, and indicates the first place of privilege and honour. Here, "first" does not relate in any way to time; rather, it refers to rank.

In Colossians 1.16, the Son stands in the supreme place of honour in relation to creation because, as verses 16-17 explain, He is the Creator and Sustainer of all things. Not only so but, as the Firstborn, He views all creation as His inheritance: after all, He is the appointed Heir of all things (Heb 1.2), and all things are "for him" (Col 1.16). In Romans 8.29, He is "the firstborn among many brethren". Among many brethren, who are conformed to His image, He stands first in rank, by reason of His unique and eternal sonship. In Colossians 1.18 (see also Revelation 1.5), He is "the firstborn from the dead"; He stands first in rank in the sphere of resurrection. We will study this statement in more depth in due course.

Having introduced the relationship of the Son to creation, the apostle justifies his previous statement by detailing five aspects of the activity of the Son in relation to "all things":

1. All things were created *in* Him (1.16, RV)
2. All things were created *by* Him (1.16)
3. All things were created *for* Him (1.16)
4. He is *before* all things (1.17)
5. All things consist *by* Him (1.17)

1. All things were created in Him (1.16)

The first statement is "for in him were all things created" (1.16, RV). This implies that the Son is the Originator of creation. Let us explore this further. In what sense were all things created "in him"? When we think about God creating, we often focus on God's power, which is, of course, vital. Yet, before the exercise of God's power, there must be the activity of His heart and mind. God's power has to do with 'how' He created, but the exercise of God's heart and mind devised 'what' He created. The Son, in His own heart and mind, conceived and designed all that He subsequently brought into being through His own power. This is truly breathtaking. All created things were first conceived and designed by the Son. The God who is eternal, conceived of time; the God who is spirit, conceived of space, energy and matter. The Son who lives, conceived of, and designed, all living creatures, whether physical or spiritual. Even our present, incomplete knowledge of the physical universe shows the incredible complexity and beauty of creation, which finds its origin in the heart and mind of the Son. This gloriously displays the unparalleled creativity and capacity of Christ. In this sense at least, all things were created "in him". Furthermore, in bringing into existence what He had conceived and designed, the Son did so without external resource; He created "all things" in His own inherent power. He was personally sufficient to do so completely and perfectly, therefore, again, all things were created "in him". Surely, with such truth before us, we can only bow and worship the Son of the Father's love, and gladly own that in all things He must have the pre-eminence.

While we can appreciate the glory of Christ here without any detailed understanding of the system of error faced by the Colossians, some knowledge will explain why Paul covers certain points. Gnostic teaching drew from the philosophy of Plato, who taught that a supreme God (because of there being a vast gulf between the higher spiritual world and the lower material world) created lesser gods to whom he delegated the task of making living things on Earth.[6] Paul dismisses this speculation, showing that the invisible God can be known through the uncreated Son, in whom all things were created.

Having explored the remarkable statement that all things were created "in him", we turn to the qualifying words, "in the heavens and upon the earth, things visible and things invisible, whether thrones or dominions or principalities or powers" (1.16, RV). A three-fold classification of creation is thus given, which we can consider as follows:

- *As to Location or Realm* – "in the heavens and upon the earth"
- *As to Nature* – "things visible and things invisible"
- *As to Government* – "thrones or dominions or principalities or powers"

The greater part of "all things" falls within the category "in the heavens". We know that there are three heavens: the heavens made on the second day, which we call the atmosphere (Gen 1.6-8); then there are the stellar heavens containing the sun, moon and stars; there is also the realm Paul called the "third heaven" (2 Cor 12.2). Each of these heavenly realms displays the fulness of the glory of the Son's creatorial work. An important observation is that each of these realms is dynamic. In the immediate heavens around Earth, birds fly, winds blow, clouds move; in each we see the wisdom of the Creator. In the stellar heavens, the moon orbits the earth, the earth orbits the sun. Relative to Earth, the constellations pass across the night sky with remarkable precision (Job 38.31-33). Indeed, the heavens are growing; what we now call cosmic expansion was revealed in Old Testament Scripture: "He that created the heavens, and stretched them out" (Isa 42.5). The present participle form of the word "stretched" allows for this stretching to be ongoing - the phenomenon which can now be observed. Again, consideration of this heavenly realm gives ample witness to the glory of the Son. Well did the psalmist write, "The heavens declare the glory of God" (Ps 19.1). What of the third heaven? Anything we know of this realm comes through revelation (not by observation or speculation). We know the identity of various spirit beings - angels, archangels, seraphims and cherubims, to name but four - all actively engaged in the service of the Creator, and all owing their existence to the Son. The realm "upon the earth" is more familiar to us and, yet again, reveals the wisdom of the Son in the varied forms of life. Again, to make the point, all this was conceived and designed by the Son, who created it all in His own power. Contemplation of this never ceases to prompt wonder in our hearts regarding the unparalleled greatness of the Son of God.

The second form of classification given is "things visible and things invisible". With the aid of a telescope and microscope, there is an incredible array of 'visible things' which we can now see. Yet, there is a realm of creation which is "invisible" – not because it is too small or too far away; it is invisible because it is a spiritual realm. (Of course, there are also physical objects which we cannot see; the reader will have heard of black holes - objects so massive that light itself cannot escape – hence we cannot see them!) What we know about the invisible living beings, both good and malign, is open to us only through the revelation of Scripture. The Gnostic had a fascination with these "things invisible", which led to vain speculation. The point made by the apostle here is that whether the things can be seen or not, they were all created in and by the Son.

The third classification delineates government in the universe. Thrones are found in relation to both earthly rule (Esth 1.2; Dan 5.20; Jonah 3.6) and heavenly administration (Rev 4.4 – the 24 "seats" are, in fact, 'thrones'). The basic idea in a throne is the seat of authority, hence it is connected with the rule of kings. Dominions are lordships, and again are found in both earthly and heavenly domains. In relation to Earth, the rule of Alexander the Great is described in these terms: "a mighty king shall stand up, that shall rule with great dominion" (Dan 11.3). The term also relates to a rank of angelic being (Eph 1.21). Again, principalities may be either a class of angelic being (Eph 1.21; 3.10; Col 2.10) or an earthly power (Titus 3.1). Recall that Michael the archangel is described as "the great prince which standeth for the children of thy people" (Dan 12.1), and that Satan is "the prince of this world" (Jn 12.31; 14.30), "the prince of the power of the air" (Eph 2.2). Finally, "powers" carries the basic thought of authorities, those who have the right to act. As with the previous terms, this applies both to earthly (Lk 12.11; Rom 13.1; Titus 3.1) and heavenly (Eph 3.10; Col 2.15; Rom 8.38) spheres. The key point is that both earthly and heavenly delegated governmental beings were created by the Son. He stands supreme in respect of government and administration over creation.

2. All things were created by Him (1.16)

This statement presents the Son as the active Cause or Agent in creation. It is He who actually brought creation into existence by the exercise of His power. As the psalmist wrote, "he spake, and it was done; he commanded, and it stood fast" (Ps 33.9). We saw earlier that Gnostic teaching drew from the philosopher Plato, who conceived of a supreme God who created lesser gods, who were delegated the task of making living things on Earth.[7] Scripture dismisses this idle speculation; it is the Son alone who created all things, whether things in the heavens or things on the earth. Nothing was too small for His attention, from the mightiest angel to the smallest insect or sub-atomic particle – He created and made them all!

3. All things were created for Him (1.16)

What is the ultimate purpose of "all things"? Scripture supplies the answer here: all things were created for the Son, for His pleasure and glory. At the beginning, God took delight in creation: "And God saw every thing that he had made, and, behold, it was very good" (Gen 1.31). This is a beautiful statement: God (the triune God) viewed the totality of what He had made and concluded it was all "very good". Additionally, God the Father has appointed Him to be the "heir of all things" (Heb 1.2); the Father has given "all things into his hand" (Jn 3.35) as a love gift. We might say that the Son has a vested interest in the ongoing existence of all things; it is His inheritance. While sin has marred this fair creation, it remains "for" the Son; He has not given up on this work, and will effect creation's full restoration (Col 1. 20).

4. He is before all things (1.17)

In simple terms, "all things" had a beginning when they were created. The Son had no such beginning; in the language of John 1.1, "In the beginning was the Word". The Word always "was". He had being, and that eternally, before He created all things. In this statement, Paul is countering a view held by many, Plato included, that God made the universe from already existing primordial chaos. If that is so, then the primordial 'stuff' from which the universe was made must be eternal. This poses considerable problems which we do not discuss here. Scripture dismisses this view with the revelation that the Son is before all things.

5. All things consist by Him (1.17)

The Son is not only the Agent in the initial creation, but He is also the active Agent in ensuring the ongoing existence of all things; all things consist through Him. Elsewhere, He is "upholding all things by the word of his power" (Heb 1.3). The word "consist" means to place together, to stand together, to cohere.[8] This is true at every scale, from sub-atomic particles to the behaviour of galaxies. He is the Author and active Cause of cohesion in the universe. Readers may wonder how this relates to what we call the laws of nature. In brief, there is consistency and uniformity as to the way in which the Son holds all things together. This means we observe order and law in creation. The formulation of this observed order is what might be termed the laws of nature. Amazingly, this is not simply qualitative but, through the abstract language of mathematics, the behaviour of the universe can be approximated quantitatively. We can predict, for example, the time it will take for Earth to orbit the sun. Yet, without the Son, no such order could pertain.

The Church (1.18) – He is the Head

Next, we view Christ in relation to the Church, which is here presented as "the body". The Church is the aggregate of all believers from the Day of Pentecost (Acts 2) to the Rapture (1 Thess 4.13-18; Jn 14.2-4). This Church is viewed in the New Testament in three ways: as a Building (Eph 2.21), a Body (Col 1.18; Eph 1.22) and a Bride (Eph 5.25-33; Rev 19.7-8). In broad terms, the Building involves the concept of stability, the Body the idea of living union, the Bride the concept of affection.

That the Church is viewed as a body shows that fellow-believers are members one of another. The focus here, though, is the relationship of Christ to the Church; He is the Head of the Church, as the head is to the body. There are three key thoughts to briefly note. Firstly, there is a spiritual union between Christ and the Church. This is of vital importance in the context of the letter; the Gnostic teachers would have introduced a distance between the believer and the Lord, suggesting that access to intermediary beings was required (Col 2.18-19). Paul counters this by showing the Colossians, and us, that we are united to Christ the Head. The second idea is that the head is to be expressed in the members of the body. This thought is captured in the words "Christ in you" (1.27), with the practical implications being detailed in chapter 3. The life of the head is to be expressed in the members of the body, and the body is to be subject to the head. The body moves under the direction and energy of the head. The third key thought is that the head supplies the need of the body, hence the exhortation of Colossians 2.19 to "[hold] the Head". Believers, in one sense, do not need to concern themselves with unseen spirit beings; we need to look directly to Christ as our Head in Heaven. There can be no doubt that Christ has the pre-eminent place in relation to the Church. This is a key doctrinal principle: the Church has one Head, Christ in Heaven. This implies that the Church has no earthly head; Christ has not delegated His headship of the Church to any other man. The reader will discern that this truth has been seriously contradicted throughout the history of the Church. We need to guard it still; nothing less than the glory of Christ is at stake.

The subject of the headship of Christ is extensively presented in the New Testament Scriptures (for example, Romans 5, a federal head; 1 Corinthians 11, the head of every man) and here, in Colossians, two aspects are presented. The headship of Christ in relation to the Church which is His Body, and His headship of every principality and power (Col 2.10).

Resurrection (1.18) – He is the Beginning and Firstborn

Next, we consider the Son as "the beginning". Two obvious questions spring to mind. The beginning of what? And, in what sense is He the "beginning"? The context suggests that this statement is, along with the title "firstborn", to be considered in relation to resurrection from the dead. This answers the first question. Next, the word "beginning" can refer to priority in time, but also of originating power. It might be objected that the Son was not the first to rise out from among the dead, though we believe that all who experienced resurrection prior to the resurrection of Christ subsequently died a second time. However, it is certainly true that the Son was the first to rise never to die again. This blessed truth is conveyed in a number of Scriptures: "knowing that Christ being raised from the dead dieth no more" (Rom 6.9); "I am he that liveth, and was dead; and, behold, I am alive for evermore" (Rev 1.18). He is also the "beginning" in relation to resurrection because He is the Origin of the power required to raise the dead. The dead cannot raise themselves; they require an external source of power, the power of God through the Son to effect resurrection. This was evidenced in the life of the Son on Earth, raising Jairus's daughter (Lk 8.55), the widow's son (7.11-17) and Lazarus (Jn 11.43-44). Also, as noted by Paul, He was "declared to be the Son of God with power, according to the spirit of holiness, by the resurrection of the dead" (Rom 1.4, RV). As He said, "I am the resurrection, and the life" (Jn 11.25). Again, it will be His "shout" (1 Thess 4.16) which will raise the dead in Christ at His coming to the air. We can say that He is the Initiator of resurrection from the dead; without Him it could not happen.

He is also the "firstborn from the dead" (Col 1.18). As we have seen, the title "firstborn" denotes rank and honour. In the sphere of resurrection, the Son has a place of unique honour. There are at least three reasons for this.[9] In addition to Him being the power to effect resurrection, His death was unique. Death had no claim on Him, due to His sinless perfection, yet He died voluntarily. As Peter put it on the Day of Pentecost, "it was not possible that he should holden of it" (Acts 2.24). Having accomplished the will of God in life and death, His resurrection was a moral necessity as far as God was concerned. In resurrection, He thus has a unique place of honour. Secondly, as we have already noted, He was the first to rise from the dead never to die again. Thirdly, He is the only person to rise from the dead in His own power. This is the focus of the presentation of His resurrection in John's Gospel (Jn 2.19; 10.18).

The apostle's conclusion to this thrilling presentation of the Son is that "in all things he might have the preeminence" (Col 1.18). We have seen in relation to revealing God, in relation to creation, in relation to the Church and resurrection, the Son indisputably has the first place. He has no rival! The basic effect of the error to which the Colossians were exposed was to diminish Christ, to rob Him in the hearts and minds of the saints of His true place. This positive presentation of truth should enable the saint to detect the error, no matter how cleverly or cunningly presented.

The justification for the apostle's claim in verse 18 is further substantiated in verse 19: "For it pleased the Father that in him should all fulness dwell". We accept the reading quoted here; a more detailed discussion on variant readings and textual questions is given by T Bentley.[10] The key question is to identify the scope of the term "all fulness". This term should be distinguished from "all the fulness of the Godhead" which dwells in the Son (2.9); this is the essential fulness of deity and, as such, is not conditional on the Father's pleasure. Rather, the context in verses 14-22 details what is involved. It includes fulness with regard to redemption (v 14), fulness with regard to being the image of the invisible God (v 15), fulness with regard to being the Originator, the active Agent, the Goal and Sustainer of all creation (vv 16-17). Furthermore, it includes the fulness in Christ with regards to Him being the Head of the Church (v 18), the fulness in relation to resurrection (v 18) and, finally, fulness in the matter of reconciliation (vv 20-22). That the Father is pleased for this to be so demonstrates that there is no rivalry in the Godhead. The Father, who loves His Son, takes pleasure in "all fulness" dwelling in Him. The Gnostic would apportion out the fulness between various created beings, but Paul shows, rather, that "all fulness" is concentrated in the Son of the Father's love. The practical consequence is this: for redemption and reconciliation, we look alone to the Son; if we wish to learn of the invisible God, we look likewise to the Son. As members of the Church, which is His Body, we look to Christ our Head; for resurrection, again we look to the Son. As such, in all things He has the pre-eminence.

Reconciliation (1.19-22) – Peace has been made through His death

The focus now turns, in verses 19-22, to the important truth of reconciliation. We are indebted to the writings of Paul for this aspect of Gospel truth (Rom 5.10-11; 2 Cor 5.19-21; Eph 2.16). The basic idea in the Greek word translated "reconcile" is to change from a state and position of enmity to friendship.[11] A stronger form of the word occurs in verse 21, carrying the thought of reconciling completely. The doctrine unfolded in the Scriptures shows that reconciliation not only involves the removal of enmity on the part of man towards God, but the establishment of a relationship and the enjoyment of peace and fellowship. We must be clear: God is not, nor ever has been, man's enemy. It is man who is at enmity towards God. It is God who is seeking to reconcile man to Himself.

There are three basic observations to make before we study the verses before us from Colossians. The first is that God is the Initiator of reconciliation. This is clear from 2 Corinthians 5.19, "that God was in Christ, reconciling the world unto himself" and, again, "as though God did beseech you by us" (v 20), showing that the enmity is in man towards God, not in God towards man. Secondly, the purpose of reconciliation is to reconcile men to God, as Paul declares, "when we were enemies, we were reconciled to God by the death of his Son" (Rom 5.10). Thirdly, as the last quotation makes clear, the basis of reconciliation is the death of the Son of God.

Turning to the Scriptures in Colossians, Paul presents two aspects of the truth of reconciliation: in verse 20, the reconciliation of "all things"; in verses 21-22, the reconciliation of "you", the Colossians and, by extension, all believers. In verse 20, it is important to note that "his" and "him" refer to the Son; "himself" to God the Father. This interpretation is in keeping with our observations above, where we have seen that it is God the Father who reconciles to Himself through the sacrifice of the Son. We learn three important matters in verse 20:

- God has made peace
- God has done so "through the blood of his cross"
- God's intention is "to reconcile all things unto himself"

We must note at this juncture that "all things" is qualified by the subsequent phrase, "things in earth, or things in heaven" (v 20). Notice there is no mention of things under the earth (compare this with Philippians 2.10); unbelieving men and fallen spirit beings are evidently not reconciled. However, the earth, which is presently under the curse (Rom 8.20-22), and the heavens, presently accessible to fallen spirit beings, will be restored and brought into conformity with the mind and will of God. How can this be brought about? Firstly, God has made peace. He has taken the initiative and made peace - a peace which creation one day will share. How was this peace made?

It was "through the blood of his cross". This is the cost of peace. We have already seen from Romans 5.10 that we were reconciled to God by the death of His Son; here, reference is made to "the blood" - the sacrifice involving the death of Christ, and "his cross" - involving the manner of His death. Recall that it was men who called for His crucifixion (Jn 19.15), it was Pilate who passed sentence (v 16), and it was Roman soldiers who carried it out (v 18). The cross stands for the greatest expression of human enmity towards God. Yet, it is through the blood shed on that same cross that peace is made. What amazing grace is this! The peace so made will be known in creation, the curse will be removed from Earth, and the heavens purged from defilement and the presence of fallen spirit beings.

Verses 21-22 address the condition of the Colossians before conversion, and their reconciliation to God. There are three matters to learn:

- *The Need for Reconciliation:* "you, that were sometime alienated and enemies in your mind by wicked works" (1.21)
- *The Means of Reconciliation:* "in the body of his flesh through death" (1.22)
- *The Result of Reconciliation:* "to present you holy and unblameable and unreprovable in his sight" (1.22)

The need for reconciliation was two-fold. Firstly, the Colossians were "alienated" from God, meaning they were estranged from God and were not of the family of God. There is a similar thought expressed in the Epistle to the Ephesians: "alienated from the life of God" (Eph 4.18). Secondly, they were enemies, signifying hostility and hatred towards God in their thinking and resultant actions - the wicked works. This Scripture demonstrates what we know to be true: what men think is expressed in their deeds. Here, their thinking was against God, His thoughts and His ways. This tragic state makes clear the need for repentance in the heart of man; a man certainly needs to change his mind - about himself, about God, about Christ. A complete change in mind is required. Yet, in all of this, God is not man's enemy, but has moved in wondrous grace to reconcile such to Himself.

This has been accomplished "in the body of his flesh through death". The reference to the body of His flesh is important in at least two ways. The expression distinguishes the physical body of the Lord Jesus from His Body, the Church (Col 1.24). In addition, Paul stresses that this body is a body of flesh as to its composition. This countered the mistaken view of Gnostics that all flesh was necessarily evil, and that the spiritual sphere cannot be united to the physical. Sadly, this error remained, and was exposed again by John when he spoke of those who confessed not that "Jesus Christ is come in the flesh" (1 Jn 4.3). John dealt with this in his Gospel too; recall the statement, "the Word was made flesh, and dwelt among us" (Jn 1.14). While stressing the reality of the humanity of Christ, Paul nevertheless guarded His impeccability with the word "his flesh". While God sent His Son "in the likeness of sinful flesh" (Rom 8.3), there was absolutely no sin in "his flesh". Yet, the incarnation of Christ in flesh was not in itself sufficient to effect reconciliation; His death was also required. Thus, these Colossians, and we ourselves, gain the blessing of reconciliation through His death.

The results of reconciliation are described by three words - "holy", "unblameable" and "unreprovable" - which are true of believers "in his sight". The last expression implies that the distance has been removed. The term signifies 'right over against', and indicates that, such is the fitness conferred, the believer will be within the immediate gaze of God's eye. What will He see? As to our nature, we will be holy, with no blame that can be attached to us, with no charge that can be brought against us. Reconciled to God means that we can dwell happily in the immediate presence of God with no dread, but joy. Unlike Adam and Eve after the Fall, we will not seek to hide from the presence of God (Gen 3.8); the fitness conferred upon us is such that we are the "saints in light" (Col 1.12).

This prospect will be realised "if ye continue in the faith grounded and settled, and be not moved away from the hope of the gospel, which ye have heard" (v 23). The need for continuance is expressed both positively and negatively. Positively, they were to continue to be founded upon and steadfast in the faith - that body of doctrine received by faith, which certainly includes the doctrine of Christ as well as the doctrine of the

Gospel. Negatively, they were not to be moved from the hope which was presented to them when they heard the Gospel, a hope to which Paul had already made reference in verse 5, and which he speaks of again in verse 27: "the hope of glory". These words impress us with the gravity of the situation. The pernicious error of Gnosticism spelt spiritual disaster for those who embraced it. A man cannot hold to the Christ revealed in Scripture and Gnostic teaching simultaneously. John speaks of those who "went out from us, but they were not of us" (1 Jn 2.19). To leave "the faith" and embrace the deception of Gnostic teaching, because of the nature of this error, involved apostasy from the Christian faith with all that this involved in terms of eternal ruin. This would not be a simple case of backsliding; it would mean abandoning the Christ of New Testament revelation.

Chapter 4

Paul's Service (1.23-29)

The balance of chapter 1 is devoted to a personal account by Paul of his two-fold ministry, as we note in the Scripture detail now presented:

> If ye continue in the faith grounded and settled, and be not moved away from the hope of the gospel, which ye have heard, and which was preached to every creature which is under heaven; whereof I Paul am made a minister; who now rejoice in my sufferings for you, and fill up that which is behind of the afflictions of Christ in my flesh for his body's sake, which is the church: whereof I am made a minister, according to the dispensation of God which is given to me for you, to fulfil the word of God; even the mystery which hath been hid from ages and from generations, but now is made manifest to his saints: to whom God would make known what is the riches of the glory of this mystery among the Gentiles; which is Christ in you, the hope of glory: whom we preach, warning every man, and teaching every man in all wisdom; that we may present every man perfect in Christ Jesus: whereunto I also labour, striving according to his working, which worketh in me mightily (Col 1.23-29).

Two aspects of Paul's service are evidently mentioned: he was *a minister of the Gospel* (v 23), and *a minister of the Church* (v 25). The greater part of these verses is focused on the latter aspect. There are five matters to consider:

- Paul's Sufferings (1.24)
- Paul's Stewardship (1.25-27)
- Paul's Activity (1.28)

- Paul's Goal (1.28)
- Paul's Effort (1.29)

Paul's Sufferings (1.24)

With regard to his sufferings, Paul makes the following astonishing statement: "Who now rejoice in my sufferings for you, and fill up that which is behind of the afflictions of Christ in my flesh for his body's sake, which is the church" (v 24). It seems incongruous to speak of sufferings and rejoicing together, yet Paul found joy in the realisation that his suffering was for the benefit of the Church. It was not that he took masochistic pleasure in the experience of suffering, but he saw and rejoiced in the reason he suffered. Paul saw that there was an allotted portion of suffering for the Church as the Body of Christ; he was willing to fill this up in his experience of the afflictions of Christ. This suffering in no way contributed to the salvation of the Church, but was the consequence of representing Christ in a world that still rejects Him. It should hardly require stating that these afflictions were not expiatory, but exemplary. Just as Christ suffered under the religious leaders of Israel, for example, so too did Paul. As Christ experienced scorn, and even violence, at the hand of unbelievers, so too did the apostle. His reference to "my flesh" perhaps suggests it was the physical sufferings he experienced that were particularly on his mind. Note, too, that he uses the plural term "sufferings"; he reflects on the various physical hardships he endured for the sake of the Body of Christ.

Paul's Stewardship (1.25-27)

As a minister of the Church, Paul had received a "dispensation" (v 25). The word primarily signifies the management of a household or household affairs, and is used here to describe the particular responsibility which Paul had received from God - his stewardship. Elsewhere, the word is used to describe how God will administer the affairs of the world during the period called "the fulness of times" (Eph 1.10). There are three details regarding this 'dispensation' to consider:

- The Source of the Stewardship
- The Beneficiaries of the Stewardship
- The Substance of the Stewardship

Paul was clear as to the *source*: it was "the dispensation of God" (v 25). God had committed this responsibility to the apostle. With this in mind, it is clear from the closing verses of the chapter that Paul took this "dispensation" with utmost seriousness. We would all do well to reflect on how we regard the ministry each of us has been given to fulfil. In a very real sense, it has been given to us from God. "For you" describes the *beneficiaries* of Paul's ministry. While we are sure that Paul personally appreciated the truth he had been given, he also recognised that this was to be communicated to the saints; this he did with zeal, at great personal cost. Again, those of us who have the honour of teaching God's people do well to remember that the ability which has been given to us is for the benefit of the saints, not our own glory. The *substance* of this dispensation is:

> To fulfil the word of God; even the mystery which hath been hid from ages and from generations but is now made manifest to his saints: to whom God would make known what is the riches of the glory of this mystery among the Gentiles; which Christ in you, the hope of glory (1.25-27).

These words are certainly full of interesting truth. An obvious question is: in what sense did Paul "fulfil the word of God"? After all, the Apostle John wrote the last books of the canon, long after Paul had gone to be with the Lord. The quotation addresses our question. Paul fulfilled, or filled up, the Word of God when he revealed "the mystery" concerning Christ and the Church: Christ the Head and the Church His Body. That is, "[fulfilling] the word of God" is not referring to the completion of the canon of Scripture, which was by the hand of John, but to the revelation of the last great area of divine truth to be made known to the saints of this era. In effect, once Paul had written the Epistles to the Ephesians and Colossians, he had fulfilled this great aspect of his ministry. This is also in view in 1 Corinthians 13.10, when

Paul writes "when that which is perfect is come", where "perfect" is to be taken in the sense of being complete.

That Paul calls this "the mystery" does not infer that what he reveals is mysterious; rather, as the Scripture states, the truth was previously hidden but is now revealed. The truth of Christ as the Head of the Church, His Body, was not revealed in previous ages of God's dealings with humanity, nor to any past generation of men. This means, for example, that the patriarchs would not have known about this, nor the prophets; it was left until this Church era before God made it known. This, of course, makes this age special, and we do well to grasp the great privilege that is ours to appreciate the unique relationship the Church has with Christ and, equally importantly, that we have as being part of His Body, the Church. This truth is vital for us to comprehend: it will, amongst other things, preserve us from confounding the Church with Israel. Israel is not the Body of Christ, nor is it part of it; that privileged nation will again enjoy covenant relationship with God in the future (Jer 31.31).

The reference by Paul to "ages" is worth elaboration. This, and other similar references (for example, 1 Corinthians 2.7 and Hebrews 9.26, where "world" is the same word as translated "ages'"), make it clear that we are to view human history in Scripture as consisting of a sequence of ages - periods of time of undisclosed duration - which are marked by certain defining characteristics. These characteristics almost always involve the manner of God's dealing with men in a particular era. So, we can discern the Age of Conscience after the Fall and before the Flood, the Patriarchal Age, the Age of Law, and so on. This observation from Scripture illustrates the validity of viewing Biblical history as a sequence of 'dispensations'. The word 'age' refers to the period of time; the term 'dispensation' to the manner of God's dealings. As referred to earlier, during the period of the "fulness of times" (Eph 1.10), God will bring all things under the headship of Christ; this is how all things will be administered during Christ's Millennial Kingdom. In summary, dispensational truth is not a theological construct imposed on Scripture; rather, it emerges clearly from Scripture as the way in which God intends us to view His varied dealings with men. In particular, Ephesians and Colossians allow the believer of this age to understand where we fit into the great scheme of God's dealings, and to see what is unique to this era. This is not merely to educate the mind, but also to delight the heart. This leads naturally on to verse 27.

Verse 27 shows that God willed that the saints should know this great truth and appreciate the riches of the glory of this mystery. There is a wealth of glory associated with our union with Christ. Paul succinctly puts it like this: "Christ in you, the hope of glory". The purpose of the body is to give expression to the mind and life of the head. Our union with Christ is so that He might be expressed in us. The practical implications of this statement are unfolded in chapter 3. The Church's greatest glory now is to display in life and testimony the life and character of our exalted Head, the Man Christ Jesus. We also have the hope of glory; Paul elaborates upon this again in chapter 3 - when Christ is manifested at His appearing, we too will be manifested with Him in glory. What a prospect! This is undoubtedly a noble truth which elevates the heart and mind of the believer. It is thrilling to be part of this Church, eternally united to Christ, yet it is sobering to reflect on how unlike Christ we can be. In the uncertainty of this age, to have the sure hope that we will share in Christ's day of glory is both a comfort and a motivation to continue to live for Him and engage in service for Him now.

Paul's Activity (1.28)

Three words sum up the description of Paul's activity: preach, warn, teach. The basic idea in preaching is that of making an announcement. The subject of his preaching is captured in the word "whom" (v 28). This is both simple and important; Paul's preaching focused on Christ; he announced the Person of Christ. Here, it is not a question of *what* he preached, but *who* he preached. There is a challenge in this for every preacher: how much do we focus in our preaching on the Person of the Lord Jesus? While it is imperative to deal with the human condition and destiny, neither of these elements can be separated from the presentation of the Person of Christ. As Paul reminded the Corinthian believers, "I determined not to know any thing among you, save Jesus Christ, and him crucified" (1 Cor 2.2). Colossians chapter 1 amply demonstrates that Paul had a deep appreciation of Christ, and this he declared in his preaching.

Secondly, he was engaged in "warning every man" (Col 1.28). He made both sinners and saints aware of danger, present and future. In the context, the warning here is particularly with believers in view. Paul was acutely aware of the spiritual danger facing the Colossian saints from Gnostic teachers, a danger to which he makes direct reference in chapter 2. Before dealing with the specifics, he identifies this aspect of his ministry to the Colossians. The warning was for "every man"; he desired none to fall prey to the danger. He had such a heart for all the saints. In our day, we should be grateful for such warnings. The timely ministry regarding spiritual danger from godly men of spiritual insight is to be welcomed, not condemned; we do well to heed their warning. It should, of course, be noted that no matter the faithfulness of the servant in warning "every man", those warned need to take account of the danger and heed the warning in order to benefit personally.

Thirdly, he was engaged in "teaching every man in all wisdom" (v 28), which was very much a positive ministry. This is again evident from this very chapter, where Paul has given thrilling instruction relating to the Person and work of Christ, the truth of the Gospel, the relationship of the Church to Christ, and the believer's hope. As we move to the later parts of the letter, he further instructs in practical Christian living. These are all areas in which we need to be taught. This very epistle (as with Paul's other epistles) provides a sound model for how to go about teaching the saints. His teaching was for "every man"; again, we see the heart of the apostle for the saints; he wanted no believer to be left in ignorance. The wisdom imparted through the apostle's teaching was not that of the philosopher, as we find in chapter 2, but it was the wisdom of God, the wisdom which comes from above (Jas 3.17). A final remark before considering the goal Paul had in mind seems appropriate. Paul's ministry contained balance and variety; he both preached, warned and taught. All of these activities were required then and, undoubtedly, are required still. We thank God that the ascended Christ still gives gifts to the Church - to preach, warn and teach.

Paul's Goal (1.28)

What was Paul's purpose in all this activity? He states his goal plainly: "that we may present every man perfect in Christ Jesus" (Col 1.28). Alongside this statement we should place the words of verse 22: "to present you holy and unblameable and unreprovable in his sight". In verse 22, we have the divine presentation of the believer; in verse 28, the apostolic presentation. The idea of 'presentation' is to place beside. In verse 22, we have the outcome of the work of God, placing us before Himself suited to His presence. In verse 28, it is the desired outcome of the apostle's ministry that is in view. In one sense, nothing can be added to our standing in Christ, as Paul teaches in chapter 2: "ye are complete in him" (2.10). That said, Paul saw there was a need for the saint in Christ to mature in spiritual matters. The idea in the word "perfect" is that of being full grown,[12] mature, whether physically or, as here, in a spiritual sense. The believer needs to grow. Why was this important for the apostle? Firstly, the absence of growth is unnatural! Secondly, he knew that mature believers would be less vulnerable to the cunning deceit of false teachers. Positively teaching the saints and seeing individual saints advance was the sure way to assist in the preservation of the believer. As noted previously, observe Paul's desire for this to be so for "every man". He had lofty ambitions for the saints, seeing the potential for every believer, thus he ministered tirelessly to this end. Perhaps we need to capture a fresh sense of Paul's vision here - seeking the advancement of the saints.

Paul's Effort (1.29)

This brings us to consider Paul's effort, which is described in verse 29. The verse contains two sides which need to be held in balance. On the one hand, Paul describes his activity; on the other, Christ's working in the apostle. From Paul's perspective, he engaged in "labour" and "striving". This labour is more than work; it carries the thought of toil to the point of weariness. Seeking to perfect the saints through his ministry was no easy matter; it involved the expenditure of energy, and that to such a degree that he would feel wearied. Consideration of the itinerant life of the apostle makes it clear that it placed considerable physical, emotional and mental stress on him. We should not dismiss this in the present. For the teacher, long hours must be spent over the Word of God, often considerable time is spent in travel to visit assemblies, and then there are the physical and emotional demands of preaching. This vital ministry involves labour yet!

Paul adds a second word: "striving". The verb is used of contending in public games (1 Cor 9.25), of engaging in conflict (Jn 18.36) and, metaphorically, to contend perseveringly against opposition and temptation (1 Tim 6.12; 2 Tim 4.7). The word is that from which we get the English word 'agonise'. The apostle conveys a real sense of struggle and inner burden about these matters. Above all, and using a modern term, Paul realised that the stakes were high! Not only was the glory of Christ at stake, but also the spiritual welfare of the saints. With this inner realisation, he gave himself to his ministry, even when this involved opposition, as it often did for Paul. We need to recognise that the ministry of preaching, warning and teaching takes place in enemy territory. The truth will be contested. In the face of such opposition, one might echo the question, "who is sufficient for these things?" (2 Cor 2.16). Colossians 1.29 supplies the answer: Christ is! Paul was careful to recognise that, although his service meant for him labour and striving, it was "according to *his working*, which worketh in me mightily" (v 29). As he stated in a different context, "I can do all things through Christ which strengtheneth me" (Phil 4.13). Here is the other important side to divine service: it is Christ working in His own power through His servants. The service of preaching, warning and teaching was, in fact, a divine work, carried forward in the power of God. Paul knew what it was to rely on divine enabling in his ministry.

In summary, God gave Paul a ministry to fulfil; He also empowered him to fulfil it. On the other hand, Paul was willing to spend and be spent, labouring and striving. There is an obvious application to us. We need to come to understand the service God has entrusted to each of us, then to depend on Christ to enable us to fulfil that service, being vessels through whom the Lord is working, recognising this will involve labour, and perhaps striving, on our part.

Chapter 5

Prelude to Chapter 2

Reading through Colossians chapter 2, one may be excused for thinking that it is not the most straightforward section of the New Testament to understand. The reader may have made a mental note of a number of statements throughout the chapter requiring further explanation. While this may be so, we should not be discouraged from seeking to grasp the important truths conveyed by Paul in these verses. This illustrates a simple but vital point: not all Scripture is easy to understand, but all Scripture is there to be understood. The Apostle Peter later observed of Paul's writings, "speaking in them of these things; in which are some things hard to be understood" (2 Pet 3.16). While there may be things "*hard* to be understood", this does not imply that such things *cannot* be understood. We must hold to the promise of 2 Timothy 2.7: "Consider what I say; and the Lord give thee understanding in all things". In such cases, a good approach is to look for key statements and overall structure, before focusing on particular details.

Reading through chapter 2 again (and the author encourages the reader to do just that), there are three basic observations which can be readily made:

1. Paul was deeply concerned for the spiritual wellbeing of the saints at Colosse. This is apparent from verse 1: "I would that ye knew what great conflict I have for you".
2. Paul made the Colossians aware of the present danger they faced. This is evident from the following quotations:
   - "This I say, lest any man should beguile you with enticing words" (2.4)

- "Beware lest any man spoil you through philosophy and vain deceit" (2.8)
- "Let no man therefore judge you in meat …" (2.16)
- "Let no man beguile you of your reward" (2.18)
- "Why, as though living in the world, are ye subject to ordinances?" (2.20)

3. The preservation of the saints was to be found in an appropriate appreciation of the Person and work of Christ, and our spiritual union with Him. This is evident from the abundant references in the chapter to a wide variety of truths relating to the Lord Jesus.

Putting these together, we immediately see that the chapter is about apostolic concern, warnings of spiritual danger, and the means of preservation for the saints in the face of such danger. Further insight can be gained by observing the structure of the apostle's argument. In verses 1-10, Paul warns the Colossians of the dangers associated with philosophy. There are two warnings to be heeded. In verse 4, the warning regarding "enticing words" has to do with the method employed by the false teachers; in verse 8, the reference to "philosophy" focuses on the substance of the false teaching. In verse 4, the *method*; in verse 8, the *matter*. We will return to consider in some detail the precise nature of the danger posed by philosophy.

Reading into verse 11 and beyond, the reader will readily detect a strong Jewish flavour to the matters raised by the apostle. There is reference to circumcision (v 11), the Law (v 14), Jewish ritual (vv 16-17) and angels (v 18). The warnings in this section embrace two extremes. In verse 16, Paul warns against *Jewish ritual*; in verse 18, against a form of *Jewish mysticism*. Finally, the closing four verses of the chapter focus on a third element of danger: he warns here of asceticism, which was of Eastern origin. Gathering these observations together, we might divide the chapter as follows:

- Preservation from Philosophy and Deception (2.1-10)
- Preservation from Jewish Ritual and Mysticism (2.11-19)
- Preservation from Eastern Asceticism (2.20-23)

At this juncture, it is important to note the following: in this chapter, Paul is not refuting three errors, but one. This error, Gnosticism, drew together aspects of Greek philosophy, Jewish ritual and mysticism, and Eastern asceticism. The structure of this chapter reflects the three main elements of Gnostic teaching; Paul breaks the error into its component elements and deals with each in turn. In doing so, he provides a good model for us. Error may not always be simple to refute. Identifying the components and dealing with each in turn is a good method.

Describing Gnosticism is by no means simple, not least because various Gnostic sects held a range of views, which were not always mutually compatible. For information, Neander[13] describes two main strands of Gnostic teaching - the Alexandrian and Syrian schools. In simple terms, the Alexandrian school placed greater focus on the philosophical aspects; the Syrian school on the Eastern ascetic aspects. We will remark further on the nature of the threat posed by Gnostics as we proceed through the chapter.

Chapter 6

Preservation from Philosophy and Deception (2.1-10)

In the Scriptures below, it is important to note the approach adopted by the apostle. We will observe both a warning and the expectation of further spiritual progress. Continuing to make spiritual progress is a sure way of being preserved from false ideas originating in the wisdom of man.

For I would that ye knew what great conflict I have for you, and for them at Laodicea, and for as many as have not seen my face in the flesh; that their hearts might be comforted, being knit together in love, and unto all riches of the full assurance of understanding, to the acknowledgement of the mystery of God, and of the Father, and of Christ; in whom are hid all the treasures of wisdom and knowledge. And this I say, lest any man should beguile you with enticing words. For though I be absent in the flesh, yet am I with you in the spirit, joying and beholding your order, and the stedfastness of your faith in Christ. As ye have therefore received Christ Jesus the Lord, so walk ye in him: rooted and built up in him, and stablished in the faith, as ye have been taught, abounding therein with thanksgiving. Beware lest any man spoil you through philosophy and vain deceit, after the tradition of men, after the rudiments of the world, and not after Christ. For in him dwelleth all the fulness of the Godhead bodily. And ye are complete in him, which is the head of all principality and power (Col 2.1-10).

This section might be summarised under the following headlines:

- Concern for the Colossians Expressed (2.1)
- Conditions Conducive to Preservation (2.2)
- Christ, The Treasury of Wisdom and Knowledge (2.3)

- Cunning Methods of the False Teachers Exposed (2.4)
- Commendation of the Colossians (2.5)
- Continuance in Christ (2.6-7)
- Character of Philosophy (2.8)
- Christ's Fulness (2.9)
- Completeness in Christ (2.10)

Concern for the Colossians Expressed (2.1)

In verse 1, the apostle's concern is expressed in touching terms. "I would that ye knew" conveys the thought that Paul wanted the Colossians to know how much he cared for them and was concerned about them. The depth of his interest is clear in the expression, "what great conflict I have for you". The word "conflict" expresses the thought that Paul agonised over the Colossians, burdened about the dangers they faced. Clearly, this letter was written by a man deeply exercised for the Colossian saints, though it seems he had never met them personally. This 'agony' was not for the Colossians alone; he felt similarly for the saints in Laodicea and, indeed, for all who had "not seen [his] face in the flesh". The largeness of the apostle's heart for the preservation and welfare of the saints is evident. It must have been a real encouragement for the Colossians to know that a man of the spiritual calibre of Paul was so concerned for them, and in such a deep way. The example of the apostle is worthy of imitation. A respected elder or teacher saying "I want you to know how much I care for you" can uplift both an individual saint or a whole assembly unsettled by satanic deception.

Conditions Conducive to Preservation (2.2)

Paul's approach in this section is most instructive, particularly in verse 2, where he presents three conditions which are conducive to the preservation of believers. These can be summarised as follows:

- The Comfort of Mutual Love
- The Confidence Through Understanding
- The Comprehension of the Mystery of God

He desired "that their hearts might be comforted, being knit together in love". The unity of the saints in their mutual love for one another has an important part to play in their preservation. Hearts that are encouraged by the enjoyment of the mutual love of fellow-saints are less likely to fall prey to apparently attractive alternatives. This point must not be overlooked. The tragic fact must be acknowledged: it is when believers feel unloved by their fellow-saints (whether this is true or not) that the temptation arises to look beyond the assembly for alternatives. Such believers may then become vulnerable to the enticing words of false teachers.

That said, the love of fellow-believers alone is not sufficient. There must also be "the full assurance of understanding". This is most interesting; confidence here comes through understanding. This, too, is an important part of our preservation from error. We need to understand the truth and, in so doing, form a confidence in it and conviction about it. Paul prefaces this thought with the words "all riches", which implies there is a great wealth of truth to understand, and in which to have confidence. How do we arrive at such a state? It requires a personal engagement with the truth of Scripture. While we can gain knowledge from others, understanding requires a personal exercise to see how the elements of the truth interlock, and to form convictions about the veracity of what we hold by faith. This full assurance is vital in the face of the potentially unsettling attacks of error. To see this, consider the situation where such assurance of understanding is absent. For such an individual, the differing views are reduced simply to a matter of opinion, with either side of opposing views having equal validity. When the doctrine of Scripture on the one hand, and the wisdom of men on the other, are held as equals, the individual is on the slippery slope to spiritual disaster.

Christ, The Treasury of Wisdom and Knowledge (2.3)

The third and the key element in the preservation of the saints is "the acknowledgement of the mystery of God, and of the Father, and of Christ; in whom are hid all the treasures of wisdom and knowledge" (vv 2-3). This expression certainly requires some consideration. The *Revised Version* rendering is helpful: "that they may know the mystery of God, even Christ, in whom are all the treasures of wisdom and knowledge hidden". The word "mystery" is to be understood in the usual way we find in the New Testament, that is, it refers to what was previously hidden but is now revealed. The term "of God" has two potential meanings. It could infer that this mystery comes from God. Whilst this is true, the same can be said of other mysteries in the New Testament, so it seems strange to identify this particular one in these terms. We are certainly reliant on God revealing certain matters to us, which otherwise we could not know. This was the case in chapter 1 verse 27, which refers to the unique relationship between Christ and the Church. A second possibility, which we suggest is preferable, is that the mystery here relates to God Himself. That is, what was previously hidden regarding God has now been revealed. This is certainly consistent with what follows: "even Christ"; He is the Person who has fully revealed God and, as we will learn in verse 9, "in him dwelleth all the fulness of the Godhead bodily". That the Lord Jesus has given to us a full revelation of God is taught elsewhere, as the reader will no doubt recall. To cite but two examples: "No man hath seen God at any time; the only begotten Son, which is in the bosom of the Father, he hath declared him" (Jn 1.18); "he that hath seen me hath seen the Father" (14.9). Paul's desire is that the believers might have a full knowledge of God, who has been revealed by Christ. While subjectively our knowledge is limited, it can, and should, be full, extensive and growing. Instead of heeding the pretentious claims of Gnostics to higher knowledge, the apostle wants the believer to enjoy the treasury of wisdom and knowledge which resides in Christ. The believer needs no other resource; Christ alone is sufficient, being the repository of wisdom and knowledge.

This leads us to consider the following: Christ meets every human need. We have no doubt He meets our spiritual and emotional needs; we revel in His love for us. But He is also sufficient to meet our intellectual needs. The greatest human mind can find its satisfaction in the fulness of wisdom and knowledge treasured up in Christ. None would doubt that Paul himself was a man of great intellect, yet his longing was "that I may know him" (Phil 3.10). God, revealed in Christ, is such that we can never exhaust the fulness of what we can know of Him. Of course, this knowledge is not an end in itself; it should produce worship in our hearts and conformity to Him in our lives. The point at stake here is that the believer has no valid justification for leaving Christ in order to pursue so-called higher knowledge in the vain speculations of the Gnostic. Revelation in Christ excels human wisdom every time.

Cunning Methods of the False Teachers Exposed (2.4)

Verse 4 describes the cunning methods employed by the false teachers: "And this I say, lest any man should beguile you with enticing words". The possibility of the believer being deluded by the persuasive arguments of the false teachers is mitigated by the positive factors we have found in verses 2 and 3. An argument presented with "enticing words" might be persuasive, and even attractive, but this does not establish its truth. The heart of the matter is this: God can be known by every believer in the revelation in Christ, not by speculations of Gnostics. There is an important practical lesson here: there is a very real danger of believers being swayed by appealing presentation, which overrides our critical faculties when we should be alert to the dubious nature of the substance of what is being presented to us. Clever rhetoric, amusing anecdotes, or even emotional appeals, are no substitute for truth. Whilst being able to present the truth of God in an interesting and simple manner is important for every teacher, the mode of presentation should not detract from the substance of what is being taught.

Commendation of the Colossians (2.5)

While the Colossians faced a very real present danger, Paul was able to commend them on two counts, expressed in verse 5: "For though I be absent in the flesh, yet am I with you in the spirit, joying and beholding your order, and the stedfastness of your faith in Christ". Paul identifies the order seen in the assembly, and their faith, as items for commendation. Before commenting further on these, note the expression of Paul's interest in the Colossians. Though physically absent from them, he assures them of his solidarity with them in the words, "yet am I with you in the spirit". What an encouragement this should have been. The Apostle Paul was standing with them! He was standing in solidarity with the Colossian saints against the Gnostic teachers. The expression is not to be regarded as mystical; rather, it infers that Paul had the Colossians in his heart and mind; he was praying for them (1.9), and seeking to strengthen them through the words of this letter. For the Colossians, to know that the Apostle Paul was standing with them ought to have fortified their resolve to stand fast in the faith. When facing danger, spiritual or otherwise, it is encouraging to know that we are not alone. We know that the Lord is with us, yet it is also helpful to have fellow-believers standing with us.

The term "your order" refers to the way in which the assembly functioned at Colosse. Their order was, in fact, divine order, otherwise Paul would not have been able to commend it. Paul found joy in the orderly function of the assembly at Colosse. The word "beholding" is interesting. We might wonder how Paul could 'behold' them when physically absent. Recall that Epaphras was with Paul at this juncture (4.12), and doubtless had recounted not only their conversion, but also the detailed activity of the assembly. Paul was able to 'behold' them through the description Epaphras had given to him, and in this he had found joy. It is so still; there is a joy in hearing of saints faithfully carrying out the pattern of assembly life presented in Scripture.

Furthermore, we might enquire as to why Paul mentions "your order" here. The fact that they maintained appropriate order in the assembly was also conducive to their preservation. Suppose that, instead, they had abandoned divine order for the ideas of men. What then? This would have allowed, in principle, the adoption of human wisdom in the sphere where divine revelation should hold sway. This immediately puts us in the place of danger. If we allow human wisdom in the ordering of the assembly, then why not allow it in the matter of knowing God? Saints whose mindset is to look to God for the ordering of the assembly are in a safer place when false claims originating in human wisdom are presented. Such should continue to look to God. Though this might not be popular in the present day, it is still true. There is spiritual safety in remaining true to the pattern of church gatherings and order presented in the New Testament. To move outside the scope of Biblical revelation in the matter of church order places us in the sphere of human wisdom. We are then reliant on what we, or others, happen to think is a good idea at the time.

The second strand to Paul's commendation is the "stedfastness of your faith in Christ". Later in this section we will encounter "the faith" (v 7). The expression "your faith" (v 5) relates to our personal trust in Christ, whereas "the faith" refers to the body of doctrine which we believe. Both are vital, and both would be compromised if the Colossians fell prey to the false teaching referred to in this chapter. Paul had given thanks when he heard of "your faith in Christ Jesus" (1.4); now he expresses his joy that this faith in Christ remained firm. The implication of these words is that Paul's ministry was preventative rather than restorative. Without question, giving heed to the claims of the Gnostics would have undermined the faith of the Colossians in Christ. Happily, this had not happened. By way of application, we must be alert to anything of the wisdom of men which shakes our faith in Christ. Young believers, in particular, need our constant prayers when facing the claims of human wisdom in all tiers of education, that they might remain steadfast in their faith in Christ.

Continuance in Christ (2.6-7)

Verses 6 and 7 deal with Paul's desire for the Colossian believers to continue and progress spiritually. Two expressions are important to observe: "in him" (v 6) and "in the faith" (v 7). The first relates to our spiritual union with Christ; the second to the body of teaching which we believe. Paul's desire is built upon seven simple elements:

- Receiving Christ
- Walking in Christ
- Rooted in Christ
- Built up in Christ
- Stablished in the Faith
- Taught in the Faith
- Abounding in Faith

Note that these seven follow the common Scriptural pattern, dividing as they do into a group of four followed by a group of three: the first four relating to Christ explicitly; the following three to "the faith".

"As ye have therefore received Christ Jesus the Lord" (2.6)

The foundation of Paul's argument is to take the Colossians back to their conversion, which he does in the expression, "as ye have therefore received Christ Jesus the Lord". The use of the word "therefore" turns attention to "your faith" in verse 5. How had they received Christ? Clearly, they had received Him by exercising faith in Him (see also Colossians 1.4). The thought in 'receiving' is 'laying hold upon'. When they first exercised faith, they laid hold upon Christ Jesus as Lord. This involved acceptance that the Man Jesus is both Lord and Christ. It included acceptance of both the humanity and deity of Christ. An alternative rendering, which stresses this thought, is "ye have received the Christ, Jesus the Lord" (JND). The key point is that their continuance was predicated upon their having received Christ in the first place. The genuineness of this event is therefore crucial; having received Christ Jesus as Lord, they were to continue with Him, accepting nothing that would diminish His exalted Person.

"Walk ye in him: rooted and built up in him" (2.6-7)

The concept of 'walking' is familiar in Paul's teaching, and it is used here in an extensive sense to include the totality of the believer's conduct. The term evidently involves movement and activity. The present tense directs our attention to the continuous activity and conduct of our lives. Paul desires that we walk in Christ. This seems a strange form of expression. How can we walk in a person? As we have noted, the term "in him" describes the union of the believer with Christ; we are viewed as being "in Christ". Here, the teaching is that we are to conduct our lives in the good of this spiritual union with Christ. Developing this thought, Christ is to become the sphere of our lives; He is to become our world, our lives are to be bound up with Him, He is to be our consuming daily occupation. Paul has this in mind when he writes in Colossians 3.4, "when Christ, who is our life …". Again, in Philippians 1.21, expressing the substance of his life, he says, "for to me to live is Christ". This is deeply challenging:

our lives are to be so focused on Christ that He becomes our world. In response to the question, "What is your life?" (Jas 4.14), we are to answer, "Christ is my life". This is the practical realisation of 'walking' in Christ.

The following two elements exemplify resultant aspects of this spiritual union with Christ. Firstly, the believer is "rooted" in Him. The grammar implies that the believer has been firmly rooted in Him, which indicates abiding security and stability. The term is used as a metaphor for a building resting securely on a solid foundation. Christ is the solid foundation of our lives, due to our union with Him. Paul is the great example of this: imprisoned, denied of much that he previously enjoyed, he found that Christ was the single constant in his life. He might be denied his freedom, but no-one could rob him of his union with Christ.

While stability is vital, there is also the thought of advancement conveyed in the expression "built up in him". Again, the present tense implies a continual process of building up. Our union with Christ introduces us to a sphere where continual spiritual growth and development can take place. The believer need not look beyond Christ to find fulfilment or growth; it is the natural result of walking in Him. As we occupy ourselves with Christ, we grow in our knowledge of Him, and practically in our likeness to Him. This is spiritual growth. The Gnostics might suggest that advancement was through philosophy and speculations, but the apostle shows otherwise; it is through the believer's union with the Lord Jesus. While Paul deals with the sphere of building up, Jude, in his epistle, stresses personal responsibility: "building up yourselves on your most holy faith" (Jude v 20). Each believer is to take responsibility for their own "building up"; this not only includes personal reading and study of the Scriptures, but also taking advantage of opportunities to hear the Word of God taught.

The final three elements now focus on "the faith" - the body of doctrine which we have received by faith, and hold by faith.

"Stablished in the faith, as ye have been taught, abounding therein with thanksgiving" (2.7)

The word "stablished" carries the thought of being made firm. J N Darby translates it "assured", with the marginal suggestion "confirmed".

Paul desired that the Colossians had assurance regarding the matters they had believed; that they were convinced of the truth of those matters, and formed a firm conviction in relation to the substance of "the faith". Personal conviction is vital in the face of error; Satan will see to it that "the faith" is contested, and by that means will detect who really believes! That said, what we believe needs to be firmly grounded in the Scriptures; we need to have an accurate understanding of the faith. To believe what is untrue is evidently unhelpful, and ultimately harmful.

This leads naturally to the next element: "as ye have been taught". The Lord has graciously provided for the need of His saints to come to a knowledge and understanding of the truth through teaching in the assembly. He has also fitted men to teach His people. This teaching is vital in view of the error to which believers may be exposed. We, as His people, need to be able to distinguish between truth and error. Positive teaching informs the believer of our relationship with the Godhead, our blessings, and our responsibilities. As a consequence, the same teaching protects us from following error. As Paul considered the Colossian assembly, he was confident that they had already been taught; however, they needed to have an unshakeable conviction regarding the truth of that teaching. There is a practical lesson to note. The positive teaching of Scripture not only encourages and builds up the saints, but is also necessary for their protection from error. It is the responsibility of elders to ensure that this takes place in the context of the assembly. Furthermore, teaching needs to be consecutive and wide-ranging.

The final element in this rich, compressed, pair of verses is "abounding therein with thanksgiving". The faith provides the material for unlimited increase in knowledge and understanding. Believers, after a lifetime of studying the Word of God, realise that they have so much more to explore and know. Far from being limited and stifling, the faith opens up vast opportunities for exploration. Paul aptly mentions "the deep things of God" (1 Cor 2.10), depths which we will never exhaust or fully plumb, no matter how much time we spend in considering the truth of Scripture. This is not frustrating, but fulfilling. The faith offers the believer opportunities for growth and vitality in its unlimited fulness, taking character from the God who is its source and substance. The Gnostic had nothing of such fulness to offer. Abounding in the faith, while leading to increased knowledge and understanding, also leads the heart to God in thanksgiving. Growing in the faith leads to increase, and fresh expressions, of thanksgiving to God.

In periods of restriction, such as the apostle was experiencing in prison, perhaps we can take the opportunity to abound in the faith with thanksgiving. Not only will this lead to our spiritual preservation, but we will find it to be deeply fulfilling and enriching. We need not give our ear to the speculations of man's wisdom; we have something altogether more excellent: "the faith which was once [for all] delivered unto the saints" (Jude v 3).

In summary, there are two great principles for us to follow. We are to live in the good of our union with Christ, and be assured and fixed in the faith we have believed. We are also to continue to grow spiritually and abound in our grasp of the faith, resulting in expressions of thanksgiving to God.

Character of Philosophy (2.8)

Paul now turns his attention to warning the Colossians regarding the dangers of philosophy: "Beware lest any man spoil you through philosophy and vain deceit, after the tradition of men, after the rudiments of the world, and not after Christ".

At the time of Paul's writing, the danger was a present one for the Colossians, which is made clear by the use of the present tense of "beware". Paul was also concerned that the status of a particular false teacher would adversely influence the saints; hence, he stresses "lest any man", no matter his status, qualifications or claims. This remains important for us today; philosophy and persuasive men are still a danger to the unwary saint. The effect of embracing this particular form of error would be that such false teachers "spoil you through philosophy and vain deceit". The idea in the word "spoil" is to lead away captive as prey, from the freedom of truth to the slavery of error. While the false teaching to which the Colossians were exposed might have had substance, it was nothing but "vain deceit"; it was an empty deception, there was no truth in it. This is strong language indeed, and one might wonder precisely what kind of error could have had such an impact on the Colossian saints. To explore this further, we need to investigate the nature of philosophy.

We start with a simple question: what is philosophy? The word itself is a compound of two Greek words, *philos* (love) and *sophia* (wisdom).[14] A philosopher, then, is a lover of wisdom. The man commonly credited for coining the word, whom some readers may remember hearing of in their school days, was Pythagoras.[15] Rather than claiming to be a wise man, Pythagoras modestly claimed to be a philosopher, a lover of wisdom. This all sounds fairly innocuous; surely, should we not all be lovers of wisdom? Indeed. The real issue lies in the source of this wisdom. The danger lies in the fact that the wisdom in question originates with men, and is derived only from the "rudiments of the world"; it is "not after Christ", and revelation plays no part in it. We will comment on these statements more fully later. As an academic discipline, philosophy has many branches. To cite two examples, 'epistemology' is the inquiry into what can be known, and how we can be certain that what we know is true. It is the theory of knowledge. 'Metaphysics', on the other hand, deals with questions of being, and the relationship of mind and matter. There is nothing amiss in considering these questions, but the issue lies in how we do so, and where we turn for the answers.

Over the centuries, many schools of thought have emerged. Two schools of philosophy are cited in Acts 17.18 - the Epicureans and the Stoics. Let us note what these schools held. The Epicurean school was founded by Epicurus (342-270 BC), who taught that the aim of life was the pursuit of pleasure and happiness, thus negating fear of any 'afterlife' and its implications. Epicurus hated religion, which he claimed only produced the fear of death and, hence, diminished happiness. He claimed that the gods were remote, and had no real interest in the affairs of men. Epicurus was essentially a materialist, claiming that the universe originated by chance, and its evolution was by random movements of atoms. In that sense, he differed little from some modern atheistic thinkers. He held that the soul was material, and that it ceased to exist at death. It is amazing that many of his misconceptions are still with us today!

The Stoics, however, had a very different view of the world, one that was essentially pantheistic. They believed that all things formed part of nature, which was governed by fixed laws. They held that God and the world were not separate; God was the soul of the world. This view, then, denied that God is distinct from the world around us. The Stoic taught that the world had no beginning, but was in a continuous cycle of dissolution and creation. In this scheme, man has to accept his fate according to the divine will, as it is unfolded in nature. This causes obvious problems regarding the will of man, and leads to a fatalistic outlook.

These two examples amply illustrate the expression, "after the tradition of men, after the rudiments of the world". The men Paul encountered in Athens were following the teaching of a man or men who lived some hundreds of years before; their philosophy was "after the tradition of men". It was, at best, the wisdom originating in another man. Their view of the world was limited to the "rudiments", or elements, of the world, some of which could be observed, but many of which were simply idle speculation. In contrast, the Colossian saints had received divine revelation, given by the very Creator of the universe, who is the image of the invisible God (Col 1.15).

The particular philosophy endangering the Colossians was neither Epicurean nor Stoic; rather, it originated with the Greek philosopher Plato. In the complex error of Gnosticism, Plato's cosmology provided an overarching framework. Simply put, Plato envisaged a supreme God who made lesser gods, who then made created beings such as men. There was, then, a vast gulf between the higher spirit world and the lower material world. Into this gulf, Gnostics speculated the existence of hosts of intermediary beings, chiefly angels. They erroneously claimed to have access to a higher knowledge of the spirit world by means of angels (2.18). From the standpoint of the Gnostic, the Person of Christ posed a huge problem. The fact that God was manifest in flesh, which some Gnostics regarded as essentially evil, negated the Platonic view of this supreme God. Instead of being distant, God came so close to the material world that, in the Person of the Son, He became flesh. This effectively destroyed the Gnostic framework in one stroke. To counter this, Gnostics sought to diminish the glory of Christ in various ways: denying the relationships in the Godhead, denying the absolute deity of the Son, and denying His true humanity, to mention but three key elements of their error. The Apostle John identified these three elements in his epistles (1 Jn 2.22-23; 4.2; 2 Jn v 7), and countered them by presenting historical evidence in the Gospel which bears his name.

The key question for the Colossians, and for us, is, which doctrine is true? The Christian points to the historical account of the life of Christ, fulfilled prophecy, abundant miracles, and the resurrection as convincing evidence of the truth of the claims of Jesus Christ. The Gnostic had no such evidential base. The simple fact is, if Jesus Christ is who He claimed to be, then Gnosticism as a system of belief is false and a deception. The potential danger for the Colossians was to countenance some sort of synthesis of Christianity into the Gnostic framework. This could only happen by denying the essential glories of the Person of Christ, hence the stress that Paul placed on these truths in chapters 1 and 2 of his letter. The Apostle John is clear about the character of those who deny those glories: he calls them "antichrist" and "a liar" (1 Jn 2.22). Of those who once numbered themselves with true believers, he wrote "they went out from us, but they were not of us" (v 19).

The stress Paul places on knowledge and the truth in the Colossian epistle is to be viewed against the background of the pretentious claims of Gnostic teachers, who claimed access to higher knowledge. Such claims are illusory; it is the believer in the Lord Jesus who has access to "all the treasures of wisdom and knowledge" (Col 2.3), and each believer is able to "[increase] in the knowledge of God" (1.10). The aspiration to grow in knowledge is commendable, and the believer can fulfil these desires in union with Christ, not by giving their ear to the deception of the Gnostic. There can be no higher knowledge than the knowledge of God Himself. This is the essence of eternal life as expressed by the Son: "And this is life eternal, that they might know thee the only true God, and Jesus Christ, whom thou hast sent" (Jn 17.3). Paul's testimony is aptly summarised in Philippians 3.8: "Yea doubtless, and I count all things but loss for the excellency of the knowledge of Christ Jesus my Lord". May we have the same holy desires to know our Lord and

Saviour Jesus Christ. The teaching of this epistle is that we can, but not by resorting to the empty claims of man's wisdom. It is only available to us in Christ.

It will be noticed that Paul is not specific in this passage about the particular school of philosophy he has in mind. As we have noted, there was a specific philosophy behind the teaching of Gnosticism, but the warning here is more general. It is a warning against accepting the wisdom of men, rather than relying on the wisdom of God, given by revelation and now found in Scripture. This is a real danger today in many aspects of testimony. We are being encouraged by some to 'think outside the box', which generally means we move outside the pattern of New Testament revelation, and accept the latest ideas of men – which are simply an expression of man's wisdom. We have been warned that God will "destroy the wisdom of the wise, and … bring to nothing the understanding of the prudent" (1 Cor 1.19). This warning most certainly still applies today.

Christ's Fulness (2.9)

In verse 8, Paul presents a warning in relation to philosophy; in verses 9 and 10, he sets forth a positive declaration of truth in relation to Christ. These two verses contain three distinct statements:

- "In him dwelleth all the fulness of the Godhead bodily" (2.9)
- "Ye are complete in him" (2.10)
- "Which is the head of all principality and power" (2.10)

The first evidently relates to Christ and the Godhead, the second to Christ and the believer, and the third to Christ and two named classes of spirit beings. Together, these three statements annul the false claims of the Gnostic.

"In him dwelleth all the fulness of the Godhead bodily" (2.9)
The importance of this statement is clear: it is an unambiguous declaration of the deity of Christ and is, therefore, a key text in refuting

those who deny this vital truth. That said, it is also important to observe the connection with verse 8, indicated by the word "for". Verse 9 is to be viewed as the reason for Paul's conclusion that philosophy is "not after Christ" (v 8). That is, the revelation that the incarnate Christ is God justifies the claim that the conclusions of philosophy are not consistent with the Person of Christ. The results of human wisdom are at odds with who the Lord Jesus really is.

In order to see the import of each part of this statement, we consider how the truth builds up as follows:

1. "The Godhead"
2. "All the fulness of the Godhead"
3. "In him dwelleth all the fulness of the Godhead"
4. "In him dwelleth all the fulness of the Godhead bodily"

Firstly, in considering the term "the Godhead", we need to distinguish this from the reference in Romans 1.20: "For the invisible things of him ... are clearly seen, being understood by the things that are made, even his eternal power and Godhead". The word translated "Godhead" in Romans is the Greek word denoting the attributes of God and His divine nature.[16] The word employed in Colossians 2.9 indicates the very essence of deity. When we speak of the essence of deity, we are referring to that which is essential to God, as being God. That this essence is found in Christ implies that He is God; it is a statement of absolute deity. The connection between essence and attributes is important to note: attributes are the manifestation of essence. In learning what God is like (His attributes and nature), we learn what God is (His essence). In other words, for us, appreciating the attributes of God is the way to appreciate His essential Being.

Secondly, the term "all the fulness of the Godhead" stresses that the Godhead is full, in terms of essence. There is no sense in which there is anything lacking in God's essential Being; God cannot be any more than He already is. By way of illustration, recall the three statements recorded by the Apostle John: "God is ... Spirit" (Jn 4.24); "God is light" (1 Jn 1.5); "God is love" (4.8). Such is the fulness of the Godhead, God cannot be more spirit or light or love than He already is. Furthermore, God cannot be any holier, greater, more powerful or more glorious than He already is – there is fulness in the Godhead. Additionally, this statement also implies that Christ is not part God, He is fully God, and in Him is all the fulness of God's Being.

There is an important reference to God's fulness in Ephesians 3.19: "that ye might be filled with all the fulness of God". This statement must be distinguished from the one here in Colossians. In Ephesians, Paul is teaching that it is possible for the believer to appreciate something of the fulness of God; it is communicable to men, though we certainly cannot exhaust it since we are to be filled into this fulness. References to God in the previous chapters of Ephesians help us to see aspects of what is involved. To cite but one, in Ephesians chapters 1 and 2 we learn of the fulness of God's grace: note the expressions "the glory of his grace" (1.6), "the riches of his grace" (v 7), and "the exceeding riches of his grace" (2.7).

Thirdly, "in him dwelleth all the fulness of the Godhead" shows how the fulness of the Godhead relates specifically to Christ. The word "dwelleth" implies permanence, and links absolute deity to the Person who is the Christ. Putting it another way, the office of the Christ is filled by a Person of the Godhead. Fourthly, the key word "bodily" is attached. While it is true that the fulness of the Godhead dwelt eternally in the Son prior to incarnation, the apostle now describes the situation post-incarnation. The very essence of Godhead dwells in One who has a physical body. Paul has already made reference to Christ's physical body in the statement "the body of his flesh" (1.22). Viewing the same truth from a different perspective, in becoming flesh, the Son was in no way diminished in relation to His absolute deity; all the fulness of the Godhead dwells in Him bodily. Presently, the risen, exalted Christ in Heaven has a real physical body of flesh, yet in Him dwells the essence of deity. This revelation confounds the wisdom of men. In the context of Colossians, Platonic thought postulated a vast gulf between the supreme God and the physical world. Divine revelation has brought the glorious news that not only has the supreme God come near to the material world, but the eternal

Word, who is God (Jn 1.1), became flesh. This astounding truth, which we gladly accept and rejoice in, remained a point of contention for the Gnostic; when John later wrote, he identified those who did not confess "that Jesus Christ is come in the flesh" (1 Jn 4.3).

Completeness in Christ (2.10)

"Ye are complete in him" (2.10)

Positionally, the believer is "in him", denoting our spiritual, indissoluble union with Christ. In this position the believer is complete - literally, 'filled full'. Not, it should be noted, with the fulness of the Godhead; this is not communicable. There is nothing that can be added to what we are and have in Christ which could enhance our standing before God. It is important to see that this is a statement about position or standing, not state. In terms of state, there is room for advancement; in terms of standing, each believer in union with Christ is complete before the face of God. What a blessed truth is this! Of course, we are to live practically in a way that is consistent with this standing, but the truth remains: the believer is filled full in Christ. The implication for the Colossians was that they need not give credence to those who falsely claimed to have access to higher knowledge; there is nothing and no-one higher than Christ. The believer, in union with Christ, is to have the assurance that they are viewed as being complete in Christ by God Himself. The author recalls a conversation with a 'Jehovah's Witness' in which he (the author) quoted Ephesians 1.3: "who hath blessed us with all spiritual blessings ... in Christ". The 'Jehovah's Witness' had no answer to the question, "What more can you offer me?". This is basically Paul's point: there is nothing better than union with Christ! May we appreciate and rejoice in this union.

"Which is the head of all principality and power" (2.10)

The truth of the headship of Christ is wide-ranging, as indicated below:

- Christ as a federal Head (Rom 5.12-21)
- Christ, the Head of every man (1 Cor 11.3)

- Christ the Head over all things (Eph 1.22)
- Christ the Head of the Body, the Church (Col 1.18)
- Christ the Head of every principality and power (Col 2.10)

We have already considered the headship of Christ over the Church (1.18); our attention is now directed to the fact that our Lord is also the Head of principalities and powers. "Principality and power" describes two categories of spirit beings. The term "principality" suggests one who exercises rule. Michael the archangel would seem to be among these beings: "at that time shall Michael stand up, the great prince which standeth for the children of thy people" (Dan 12.1). Here, Michael is presented as having a particular responsibility for the nation of Israel. Earlier, in Daniel 10, Michael is described as "one of the chief princes" who gave aid against the prince of the kingdom of Persia. The "power", or authorities, refers to spirit beings with delegated authority. Christ is "far above" all principality and power (Eph 1.21) and, through the Church, God is educating principalities and powers in the heavenly places in His manifold wisdom (3.10). Evidently, there are fallen principalities and powers who form part of the enemy's host arrayed against the believer (6.12). It seems likely that Paul has these same beings in mind when he teaches about Christ's victory over them in His cross (Col 2.15).

Whether good or fallen, these beings are all arrayed under the headship of Christ. Their Head is the One in whom all the fulness of the Godhead dwells bodily. There is a Man in Heaven who is their Head, whether they acknowledge this or not. Again, this truth confounds the wisdom of men; Paul ascribes Christ His proper place as Head of these spirit beings. That He is their Head places them under His authority, and demonstrates that they must move under His direction.

Chapter 7

Preservation from Jewish Ritual and Mysticism (2.11-19)

The reader will detect a marked change in tone in Colossians 2.11-19; the apostle now turns to matters which have a Jewish background. Note the references to:

- Circumcision (2.11)
- Ordinances (2.14)
- Meat and drink (2.16)
- Holyday, new moon and sabbath (2.16-17)
- Angels (2.18)

In whom also ye are circumcised with the circumcision made without hands, in putting off the body of the sins of the flesh by the circumcision of Christ: buried with him in baptism, wherein also ye are risen with him through the faith of the operation of God, who hath raised him from the dead. And you, being dead in your sins and the uncircumcision of your flesh, hath he quickened together with him, having forgiven you all trespasses; blotting out the handwriting of ordinances that was against us, which was contrary to us, and took it out of the way, nailing it to his cross; and having spoiled principalities and powers, he made a shew of them openly, triumphing over them in it. Let no man therefore judge you in meat, or in drink, or in respect of an holyday, or of the new moon, or of the sabbath days: which are a shadow of things to come; but the body is of Christ. Let no man beguile you of your reward in a voluntary humility and worshipping of angels, intruding into those things which he hath not seen, vainly puffed up by his fleshly mind, and not holding the Head, from which all the body by joints and bands having nourishment ministered, and knit together, increaseth with the increase of God (Col 2.11-19).

In this section, Paul seems to be dealing with two extremes: Jewish ritualism and Jewish mysticism. The various Gnostic sects were afflicted by these extremes to varying degrees. In terms of content, the reader will also observe that, in verses 1-10, Paul has focused on the Person of Christ and, in verses 11-19, on the work of Christ. We shall see that Paul refers to the Lord's death (v 11), burial (v 12), resurrection (v 12), quickening (v 13) and cross (v 14). In particular, the presentation of our Lord's death is most instructive. Firstly, we shall see that His death is viewed as a circumcision (v 11); later we shall learn how the claims of the Law were met by His death (v 14), and how He defeated the hosts of wicked principalities and powers (v 15). Although this was relevant to Paul's rebuttal of Gnostic teachers, for us, these Scriptures are deeply instructive in showing us the far-reaching consequences of the death of Christ. As in the opening section of the chapter, the preservation of the believer is found in an appropriate appreciation of Christ; in this case, an appreciation of His cross, death, burial and triumphant resurrection.

We now focus attention on the teaching of verse 11: "In whom ye were also circumcised with a circumcision not made with hands, in the putting off of the body of the flesh, in the circumcision of Christ" (RV). The author is sure the enquiring reader will have many questions about this interesting verse, possibly including:

- What is "the circumcision of Christ"?
- In what sense has the believer been "circumcised"?
- What is the "circumcision not made with hands"?
- What is "the body of the flesh" which has been put off?

Before proceeding with the detail, we should note that verses 11 and 12 refute the suggestion that infant baptism (or, more accurately, infant sprinkling) is the New Testament equivalent to the Old Testament circumcision. Setting aside the obvious objection that only male children were circumcised, these two verses show that the believer has already been circumcised, and is expected to be baptised. It is therefore spurious to claim that the practice of circumcising a male child on the eighth day after birth is justification for the entirely unscriptural act of sprinkling (or, as is claimed, baptising) a child, which has deluded many into thinking they were safe for eternity. In fact, this is an extreme example of failing to observe key dispensational distinctions. Let us now turn again to the text of verse 11.

The first step in understanding this verse is to appreciate the opening words, "in whom ye were also". Paul is again referring to the believer's union with Christ. This verse, then, relates again to the believer's position in Christ, an observation which sets the context for the more difficult expressions in the verse. The "whom" relates back to the Person described in verses 9 and 10, namely, Christ. In verse 10, we learned that the believer is "complete in him"; in verse 11, that in this union we are also circumcised. The word "also" is important - Paul is stressing two matters which are true of those in union with Christ. We are complete in Christ before God, and we are to understand that the "body of the flesh" has been put off. It is crucial to realise that Paul is not speaking here of something we have to accomplish; rather, these are matters we need to accept as true, and live in the light of. The nature of this circumcision is explained by the clause "not made with hands", implying that it is neither man-made nor physical. It is therefore very different from the physical circumcision found in the Old Testament. The circumcision here is a spiritual truth with practical consequences. Recall similar language in Hebrews 9.11, where the writer refers to the "greater and more perfect tabernacle", wherein Christ ministers as our High Priest, as "not made with hands".

Understanding the sense in which the believer is circumcised comes from the statement, "in the putting off of the body of the flesh". The idea in "putting off" is that of stripping off, of divesting and then discarding. What, we might ask, has been put off and discarded? The answer in the verse is, clearly, "the body of the flesh". This raises another obvious question, since we all possess a body composed of flesh, and we evidently have not put this off. The explanation is found by observing a subtle distinction. We need to distinguish "the body of *the* flesh" (RV) from the statement 'the body of flesh'; the latter simply refers to the substance from which the body is made. Reference has already been made to "the body of his flesh" (Col 1.22), referring to the physical body of the Lord, the substance of which is covered by the term "his flesh". In distinction, "the body of *the* flesh" focuses rather on the character of the body as dominated by the flesh or, to put it another way, by man's fallen nature. It is the body in this character which is to be understood as being "put off" in union with Christ. The believer's body is no longer to be the vehicle for "the flesh" but, rather, should manifest the behaviours described in some detail in Colossians chapter 3. To reiterate, it is important to realise that this circumcision is not achieved by our efforts, it is not something the believer has to do; rather, it is something the believer must accept as being true of them in Christ. Evidently, there are practical consequences to be realised in the life of the believer, but the vital point is that this verse is dealing with what we might describe as positional truth - it is true of the believer because we are in Christ. The practical consequences follow from this, and are developed by the apostle in detail in chapter 3.

How, then, was this circumcision accomplished? The answer is contained in the words, "in the circumcision of Christ". To what is Paul referring? We can quickly discount the explanation that Paul is making reference to the circumcision the Lord experienced as a child of eight days (Lk 2.21), as this circumcision was certainly made with hands and was carried out by men, whereas the circumcision of this verse was "not made with hands". Rather, reference is being made, albeit obliquely, to the death of Christ. This certainly fits the immediate context, as verse 12 speaks of the burial of Christ and then of His resurrection from the dead. Some readers may be sceptical that the death of Christ could be described as a form of circumcision. However, Old Testament Scripture foretold His death in these very terms. The reader will readily recall Isaiah 53.8, which contains the words "he was cut off out of the land of the living" - undoubtedly a reference to our Lord's death. Again, in Daniel 9.26, "after threescore and two weeks shall Messiah be cut off, but not for himself". This

Scripture forms part of the great prophecy of 70 weeks, and details precisely when the death of Christ would occur – the reader will be aware that this has been shown to have been fulfilled as prophesied. The main point for us presently is that the language of circumcision is used of the death of Christ. At Calvary, He was "cut off".

A possible objection to this explanation is that men were involved in the death of Christ, and this seems not to fit with the statement "not made with hands". It is certainly true that our Lord was crucified by men, as the psalmist records, "they pierced my hands and my feet" (Ps 22.16). Equally true, though, is that the Lord laid down His own life as an act of His own will: "No man taketh it from me, but I lay it down of myself" (Jn 10.18). Though men crucified our Lord, He laid down His own life; it is to this latter point that "the circumcision of Christ" refers. The separation of our Lord from "the land of the living" was accomplished by our Lord Himself, when He dismissed His spirit and entered into death.

In summary, we note that Paul has described two consequences of our union with Christ: we are "complete in him" (Col 2.10) and, in this self-same union, we are circumcised. In the next section, we shall see that Paul identifies three aspects of our association with Christ: in verse 12, we are "buried with him" and "are risen with him"; in verse 13, we have been "quickened together with him".

Association with Christ (2.12-13)

The idea of the believer's association or identification with Christ comes from the apostle's use of the word "with". The believer has been "buried with him" (v 12), "risen with him" (v 12) and "quickened together with him" (v 13). These statements form part of a wider collection, which includes "if ye be dead with Christ" (v 20), "your life is hid with Christ" (3.3), and "then shall ye also appear with him in glory" (v 4). These form an instructive study in their own right and, in due course, we will consider the references from chapter 3. We have observed previously the union of the believer and Christ in the statements "ye are complete in him" (2.10) and "in whom also ye are circumcised" (v 11). A consequence of this union is that the believer is seen to be identified with Christ in certain ways - in His death, His resurrection, His present life in Heaven, and His future glory. In summary, "in him" statements refer to the union of the believer and Christ; "with him" statements refer to the association of the believer with Christ. These two thoughts are not necessarily equivalent. There is an important connection though: believers are viewed in association with Christ because of our union with Him.

Turning now to the detail of the verses under consideration, the reader will see that there are four statements to consider in verse 12:

1. "Buried with him in baptism"
2. "Wherein [or, in whom] also ye are risen with him"
3. "Through the faith of the operation of God"
4. "Who hath raised him from the dead"

The first and last statements certainly relate to historical events; both the burial and resurrection of Christ are such, as was the Colossian believers' baptism. The middle two statements focus on how it is true that the believer is "risen with Christ" (3.1).

It is sometimes stated, correctly, that we are reckoned to have died with Christ when He died, and we were raised with Christ when He was raised. However, according to verse 12, we were buried with Christ when we were baptised. Our baptism, therefore, is an act of association, on the part of the believer, with Christ in His burial. This element of our association with Christ is treated differently from the others, in this respect: we needed to do something – we needed to be baptised. This stresses the importance of the ordinance of baptism; as is often said, the New Testament does not countenance an unbaptised believer. Baptism is certainly a command of the Lord (Mt 28.19-20), and this should be reason enough for every believer to be baptised. The significance of the ordinance of baptism is explained both here and in Romans 6.4. We are left in no doubt that baptism is a symbolic burial. This should also be sufficient to demonstrate that the practice of sprinkling does not equate to baptism. Sprinkling an individual with water in no way symbolises a burial, whereas immersing in water certainly does. It is a symbol, as we have seen, of our association with Christ in His burial. Evidently, burial follows death. It only makes sense for the believer to be symbolically buried in baptism, since it is already true that we "have died with Christ" (Rom 6.8, ESV). Note, and this is vital to understanding Romans chapter 6, it is not the old man that is baptised; it is the new man. To see this, we need to understand in what sense the believer died with Christ. Simply put, in Romans 6, we died with Christ *as to sin*; in Romans 7, we died with Christ a*s to the Law*; in Colossians 2, we died with Christ *as to the world*. In 1 Peter 2.24, we are seen to have died *as to sins*. Abraham first expressed the significance of burial: "give me a possession of a buryingplace with you, that I may bury my dead out of my sight" (Gen 23.4). We are to reckon in our baptism that we have been put out of sight from sin, the Law and the world, as those who have died to these things with Christ.

The reader will have observed a dualism in the apostle's doctrine. Before conversion, we lived in sin (Rom 6.2), whilst at the same time being dead in sins (Col 2.13; Eph 2.1). We might put it like this: the unbeliever is dead to God and alive to sin. After conversion, the situation is different: we are "dead indeed unto sin", while at the same time being "alive unto God" (Rom 6.11). Thus, in our baptism, viewed as a symbolic burial, we must take account of the sense in which the believer is viewed as being dead: dead to sin, dead to the Law, dead to the world.

The second clause, "wherein ye were also raised with him" (Col 2.12, RV), suggests that baptism is also a symbol of resurrection. There is, however, a textual question which requires consideration. The word translated "wherein" and "in which" by J N Darby is elsewhere consistently translated "in whom" (for example, Colossians 2.11 and Ephesians 1.7, 11, 13). This clearly changes the sense of the expression. Instead of referring to baptism, the "in whom" links back to the "him" of the previous clause. Accepting this rendering, the import of the statement is that Paul is showing how it is that we came to be raised with Christ: it is because of our union with Him. This, in turn, is linked to the following clause: "through the faith of the operation of God". That is, our union with Christ is linked to our faith, which is true whether or not we are baptised. Union with Christ, here viewed as the consequence of faith, involves the association of the believer in certain events experienced by the Lord Jesus, His death and resurrection being two such examples. Some may object to this interpretation on the grounds that it removes the significance of the emergence of the believer from the water during baptism.

As we have just noted, Paul also stresses that the individual faith of the believer is involved; we were raised with Christ "through the faith of the operation of God". This is how we came individually into the good of the death and resurrection of Christ. The particular phrasing of this expression is interesting. At first reading, one might think that the faith comes from the operation of God. This is not, in fact, the case. Rather, Paul is teaching that the faith of the believer has the "operation" or effective working of God as its object. It may be opportune to comment more broadly on the prepositions used in relation to faith. In Colossians 1.4, we have already encountered "faith in Christ Jesus". The preposition "in" or 'into' stresses *the activity of faith*. In Acts 16.31, in the well-known response to the jailer's question, Paul and Silas declared, "Believe on the Lord Jesus Christ", where the preposition "on" implies that by faith we rest, rely on, depend on the Lord Jesus Christ. We might term it *the repose of faith*. Here, in Colossians 2.12, the term "faith of" directs our attention to *the object of faith*; in this case, the operation of God. The term "operation" conveys the idea that God is effective in His working; in this case, in the resurrection of Christ from the dead. This is a precious thought; God always accomplishes His design and purpose in His actions. The exercise of God's power in the resurrection of Christ was effective; God accomplished His goal, namely, raising His Son from the dead. Scripture multiplies examples of the working of our God; we see that we can trust Him, and He always accomplishes His goal. His power is always sufficient.

We have already alluded to the final clause of the verse, "who hath raised him from the dead". The importance of this historical event cannot be over-stressed. The bodily resurrection of Christ is the historical fact which is central to the Christian Gospel (see 1 Corinthians 15.1-18, for example). Here it is viewed as being the result of the effective working of God. The sceptic in our day dismisses the reality of the resurrection of Christ on the grounds that there is no scientific explanation for this event. In one sense, they are right - there *is* no scientific explanation! The resurrection of Christ was accomplished by the direct intervention of God, providing us with a striking example of the effectiveness of His working. In this passage, we could hardly be raised with Christ if Christ had not first been raised.

In conclusion, we make one simple but vital observation. The spiritual truth of the believer's association with Christ in His death and resurrection depends on the reality of two historical events - the death and the resurrection of Christ. The Gospel is grounded in real, historical events which took place in this world; there was a time when and a place where our Lord died and rose again.

Our consideration of verse 13 focuses on four statements, stated here for reference:

1. "And you, being dead in your sins …"
2. "… and the uncircumcision of your flesh …"
3. "… hath he quickened together with him …"
4. "… having forgiven you all trespasses"

The first pair of statements describes the state of the Colossians (and us) *before* conversion; the second pair relates to two things which took place *at* conversion.

Let us now consider the first of these four statements. The importance of the expression "and you" is as follows: in verse 12, the effective working of God was seen in the resurrection of Christ from the dead; in verse 13, the same effective working has made alive those who were previously dead in their trespasses. Next, note that "sins" and "trespasses" are translations of the same Greek word *paraptoma*. In the parallel passage in Ephesians 2.1, both trespasses (*paraptoma*) and sins (*hamartia*) are mentioned. "Trespasses" refers to failure in *commission*; "sins" to failure in *omission*. The basic question to be considered is, what does it mean to be dead *in* trespasses? It is certainly different from being dead *to* trespasses.

We need to return to the first reference to death in the Book of Genesis to explore this further. Readers will readily recall God's warning to Adam regarding the tree of the knowledge of good and evil: "for in the day that thou eatest thereof thou shalt surely die" (Gen 2.17). Certainly, when Adam transgressed, God indicated that he would die physically: "… till thou return unto the ground; for out of it wast thou taken: for dust thou art, and unto dust shalt thou return" (3.19). Adam's death is thus recorded: "all the days that Adam lived were nine hundred and thirty years: and he died" (5.5). Yet, there is a sense in which Adam died on the day when he took of the forbidden fruit. In order to understand this, we must appreciate that a key element in the concept of death is separation. When Adam eventually died physically, his soul was separated from his body, which then returned to the earth from whence it had been taken. Yet, a careful reading of Genesis 3 makes clear that there was a separation the moment Adam sinned - a separation between Adam and God. There are three key indicators of this fact: an awakened conscience (they knew they were naked); a futile attempt to provide for themselves a covering (God would provide a skin, at the cost of the life of an innocent animal); their equally futile attempt to hide from the presence of God. Adam and Eve, by their actions, judged their own state before God. Their actions demonstrated that a spiritual separation had been introduced between themselves and God. Genesis 3 concludes with Adam and Eve being separated from life in the Garden of Eden. They had died to that life of innocence and joy in the paradise God had prepared for them.

The Lord Himself made reference to death in this sense when He said, "He that heareth my word, and believeth on him that sent me, hath everlasting life, and shall not come into condemnation; but is passed from death unto life" (Jn 5.24). Again, "The hour is coming, and now is, when the dead shall hear the voice of the Son of God: and they that hear shall live" (v 25). The terms "dead" and "death" in these verses are to be viewed in contrast with everlasting life. Hence, the sinner is viewed as being dead (though active in sins and in the operation of the flesh), but receives life from God at conversion.

The term "dead" in Colossians 2.13 seems to cover both sins and the "uncircumcision of your flesh". In this state of death, of separation from the life of God, the individual lives in a state dominated by the pursuit of sins and the unjudged activity of the flesh, giving expression to man's fallen nature. Into this state, God has moved with His effective operation in quickening "together with him". Here, then, is another aspect of our association with Christ. We are reckoned to have been quickened with Him. The word "quickened" means to make alive. We find the same thought expressed in Ephesians 2.4-5: "But God, who is rich in mercy, for his great love wherewith he loved us, even when we were dead in sins, hath quickened us together with Christ". With regard to the Lord Himself, Peter wrote: "being put to death in the flesh, but quickened by the Spirit" (1 Pet 3.18). This indicates the role of the Holy Spirit in the resurrection of Christ from the dead. Each Person of the Godhead, acting in perfect unity, was involved. Christ was raised by the "exceeding greatness" of God the Father's power (Eph 1.19), Christ personally had both the power and authority to take up His own life again (Jn 2.19; 10.17-18), and the Holy Spirit was involved with 'quickening'.

We now need to explore this concept of quickening and its relationship to the term resurrection or raised. That these terms are related there seems no doubt, but they are not simply equivalent. The connection might be expressed thus: quickening is necessary for resurrection, and resurrection is the consequence of quickening. It should be noted further that resurrection relates to the *body* of the individual. In the context of Colossians, we are associated with Christ in His literal, bodily resurrection. The term quickening covers the reunion of the immaterial and material parts of man's being, so that we recognise that the person is alive again. To put it another way, it involves the reuniting of body, soul and spirit. To illustrate, take the example of Lazarus in John 11. What was necessary for Lazarus to be raised from the dead? Firstly, the Lord had to return the body of Lazarus to a state consistent with life (his organs and bodily systems needed to be miraculously returned to functioning order); then the soul of Lazarus needed to be reunited with his body. Lazarus then arose and left the tomb. It was clearly recognised that he was alive again! He had been raised from the dead.

While the term 'raised' certainly includes the body of an individual, the term 'quickening' contains the spiritual dimension. In the verse we are considering, it is the imparting of eternal life to the soul estranged from the life of God. We need to remember that the life of God is essentially a spiritual concept. Indeed, the first life we encounter in Genesis is spiritual life - it is the life of the living God. Then we are introduced to the life of plants, then birds and fish, then land animals and, finally, the unique life of man.

Before moving on, note the apostle's use of the word "together". He could have simply said, 'quickened with him', but he adds "quickened *together* with him". This involves a shared life. Although we came as individuals to Christ and received life, all saints have received the same life. Thus, there is a fellowship between saints on the basis that we have been "quickened together". This is a fellowship of life, of eternal life, a life focused on God and His things. As the Son of God expressed, "this is life eternal, that they might know thee the only true God, and Jesus Christ, whom thou hast sent" (Jn 17.3).

The final clause of the verse contains the vital words, "having forgiven you all trespasses". Paul has already spoken about forgiveness in Colossians 1.14, linking it to the great truth of redemption through the blood of Christ. This verse, as a whole, shows that God has met our need fully. As those dead in trespasses, we had a two-fold need. Firstly, we needed to be made alive and, secondly, the trespasses we had committed needed to be forgiven. Only then could the conscience have peace from a sense of guilt, and we could enjoy the life of fellowship with divine Persons. Note, further, that this expression is full of certainty and assurance. God's forgiveness is viewed as an accomplished fact: "having forgiven". We are not kept in suspense as to whether or not we will be forgiven; we are forgiven! The forgiveness is also total; God graciously has forgiven "all trespasses". This shows the sufficiency of the death of Christ, and brings to the saint a deep sense of relief and gratitude to God.

How glad we should be that we are the objects of God's effective working; we have been made alive in association with Christ and have received a complete forgiveness. May this produce appropriate expressions of thanksgiving and praise in our hearts to God.

The Cross of Christ (2.14-15)

The focus of verses 14-15 is the cross of Christ. The truth of the cross is viewed from two perspectives, namely:

* The Cross and the Law (2.14)
* The Cross and Principalities and Powers (2.15)

In each verse, we find three divine actions: in verse 14, we find God "blotting out", then He "took it out of the way", "nailing it to his cross". In verse 15, God has "spoiled principalities and powers", then He "made a shew of them openly", "triumphing over them in it". Reference here seems to refer to God the Father, rather than the Lord Jesus specifically. To see this, read again from verse 12. Paul refers to the "operation of God", and then describes various matters that are the result of God's effective working, including the resurrection of Christ (v 12) and the quickening of the believer (v 13). Verse 14-15 are a continuation of this sentence, and give further examples of the operation of God.

The Law is described by the expression "the handwriting of ordinances" (v 14), and is said to be "against us", and "contrary to us". The word "ordinances" refers to a legal obligation which was a binding law or edict, placed in a public place for all to see. The word perhaps refers to a document containing such decrees. The word "handwriting" was used of a written acknowledgement of debt, a statement of indebtedness, personally signed by the debtor.[17] It seems hard to sustain this interpretation with regard to the Law of God; the demands and penalty of the Law hold, whether or not the debtor acknowledges the debt. Rather, it is suggested that the handwriting refers to what God had written; after all, this was how the Law was initially given on divinely-written tables of stone (Ex 31.18). Such a handwriting of ordinances has been publicly declared in the Old Testament Scriptures. This handwriting is "against us" - it declares the utter failure of man to keep God's Law, and it is "contrary to us" - the full penalty for failing to keep these commandments is demanded.

We now come to divine activity in relation to this "handwriting". Firstly, there has been a divine "blotting out". The word has the basic meaning of washing over or wiping out. It was used of wiping out a memory of an experience, cancelling a vote, annulling a law, or cancelling a charge or debt. The Law, which exposed man's failure and demanded that the penalty be exacted, has been removed. Only the Lawgiver could carry out such an act. That God is just in so doing is explained elsewhere, for instance, Galatians 3.13; Christ has borne the curse of a broken Law. The price for the broken Law has been paid in the sacrifice of Christ, so God is free to justly blot out the "handwriting of ordinances". He then "took it out of the way", which carries the idea of taking out of the midst. For the Jew, and certain adherents to Gnostic teaching, the ethics and ceremony of the Law were central; their life and practice revolved around Law-keeping. Here, Paul instructs the Colossians that such an outlook is now contrary to what God Himself had done at the cross - He had taken the ordinances out of the midst. This change is dramatic; the focus was no longer on a code, but on a Person, and our relationship with that Person, namely, the exalted Lord Jesus, our Head in Heaven. The importance of this truth is brought out in verse 19. Finally, by "nailing it to his cross", God has shown that He has finished forever with these ordinances. We should be glad about this. Israel convincingly demonstrated that humanity was incapable of keeping the Law and, at the same time, reduced to mere ritual ceremonial activity that which ought to have expressed their relationship to the Lawgiver. Thankfully, that era has passed. Christ in His sacrifice paid the price of a broken Law; God in the cross has finished with it.

In verse 15, the apostle turns to the cross and principalities and powers. Again, three actions of God are noted, in summary:

- Spoiling
- Shewing
- Triumphing

That the cross is still in view is inferred from the final clause, "triumphing over them in it". The "it" would seem to refer back to "his cross" in verse 14. Accepting this inference leads to an important observation. At the cross, there was a vital divine victory over spirit powers. Although principalities and powers have already been mentioned (1.16; 2.10), here it seems that Paul has in mind fallen spirit powers, such as we read of in Ephesians 6.12: "For we wrestle not against flesh and blood, but against principalities, against powers, against the rulers of the darkness of this world, against spiritual wickedness in high places". That Satan and his hosts were active at Calvary is clear from the Lord's own words: "this is your hour, and the power of darkness" (Lk 22.53). It is clear, for instance, that Satan exploited Judas in the betrayal of Jesus: "then entered Satan into Judas" (v 3). It is not hard to envisage satanic encouragement behind the response of the people and leaders of Israel when they cried, "Crucify him" (Jn 19.6, 15). Importantly, once on the cross, the voice of the people and their leaders was for Him to come down from the cross: "If thou be the Son of God, come down from the cross" (Mt 27.40); "If he be the King of Israel, let him now come down from the cross" (v 42); "He trusted in God; let him deliver him now, if he will have him" (v 43); "If thou be Christ, save thyself and us" (Lk 23.39). Could it be that Satan and his hosts were behind these voices too? There is no reason to dismiss the thought that, throughout the time the Lord was on the cross, Satan and his hosts continued vainly to abuse the Lord and to encourage Him to come down from the cross. That He did not, and that He accomplished the work of propitiation, marked a catastrophic defeat for Satan and his followers. We have further information regarding the implications of the Lord's death in Hebrews 2.14-15: "that through death he might destroy him that had the power of death, that is, the devil; and deliver them who through fear of death were all their lifetime subject to bondage".

It is well worth considering further the nature of the defeat faced by Satan and his hosts at the cross. God's blessing and salvation for man evidently rests on the basis of the sacrifice of Christ; this Satan certainly opposed. That men can now be delivered from the "authority of darkness" (Col 1.13, JND) is certainly an ongoing evidence that the "rulers of the darkness of this world [age]" (Eph 6.12) were defeated at the cross. The ultimate removal of sin rests on the sacrifice of Christ (Heb 9.26), as does the establishment of the Kingdom of God in manifestation. The Lord has purchased the world (Mt 13.44), and God's plan is set for His King to reign (Ps 2.6). Satan personally has been vanquished in the death of Christ; he no longer has the power of death, which is now in the hands of Christ (Rev 1.18). His ultimate banishment, and that of his hosts, has been secured by the divine victory at the cross. God's purpose will ultimately be realised; the work of the cross guarantees this accomplishment.

It remains to briefly consider how it can be said that "he made a shew of them openly" (Col 2.15). The basic idea in the word "shew" is to display, in the context of a victor displaying his captives or trophies in triumphal procession. How has God done this, when references to the impact of the death of Christ on spirit powers are relatively few? That Christ died publicly, that He rose from the dead with abundant witnesses and the public evidence of the empty tomb, and that He ascended to Heaven, through the domain of the enemy unimpeded, witnessed by the disciples, constitutes an openly-declared victory over Satan and fallen spirit powers. Together, they were powerless to thwart the death, resurrection and ascension of Christ. These events, including the cross, are an open declaration of God's victory.

We conclude by commenting on the fact that verses 14-15 have presented six actions of God, rather than specifically Christ, as we might have expected. Of course, Christ is God. That said, the focus here is important to observe. God gave the Law; only God can take it "out of the way". This was accomplished through the work of the cross. Secondly, satanic rebellion, and that of his fallen followers, is directly against God. God is seen to triumph over these fallen spirit powers, again in the cross of Christ. Christ endured the cross, and all that satanic powers vainly attempted to effect; He gained the victory, which can rightly be described as God's victory.

Jewish Ritual and Mysticism (2.16-19)

Two matters are dealt with by the apostle in these verses: Jewish ritual based on the ceremonial law, and Jewish mysticism. The structure of the verses is straightforward to observe:

- *Jewish Ritual* – "Let no man therefore judge you …" (2.16-17)
- *Jewish Mysticism* – "Let no man beguile you …" (2.18-19)

Dealing first with matters relating to Jewish ritual, verse 16 contains a list of five items:

- "In meat"
- "In drink"
- "In respect of an holyday [feast day]"
- "Of the new moon"
- "Of the sabbath days"

One can readily see that the list divides into two: the first two items relate to diet; the next three items have to do with the observance of time. Verse 17 provides an explanation: the items in verse 16 are "a shadow of things to come", but "the body is of Christ".

Note, first, the word "therefore" in verse 16, which provides a link back to the previous verses, notably, verse 14. In view of what God accomplished through the cross of Christ, Paul now makes the exhortation, "Let no man therefore judge you". This exhortation requires some explanation. How could the Colossians prevent men from judging them? In one sense, they could not prevent men's judgment. The sense is perhaps this: in view of Calvary, the non-adherence to the ceremonial law was not legitimate grounds for men to pass judgment on the Colossians. They were not to be adversely affected by the verdict of men, notably, those who adhered to such ritual.

Leviticus 11 provides detailed instructions for Israel with regard to what may or may not be eaten. The Colossians were no longer bound to these, though this chapter does provide profitable spiritual lessons for the believer of this age. Following a certain diet, eating or not eating certain foodstuff, did not improve or diminish the spiritual state of the Colossians. They could not attain a higher spiritual state on the ground of their diet. Recall Paul's teaching in 1 Timothy 4.4-5: "For every creature of God is good, and nothing to be refused, if it be received with thanksgiving: for it is sanctified by the word of God and prayer".

The three time-related items are said to be "a shadow of things to come" (Col 2.17) and, in contrast, "the body is of Christ". Clearly, a shadow casts an outline of the real entity, but is not that entity. So it is with the feast days, the new moon and the sabbath days; they foreshadowed future events, but were not in themselves the substance. As we shall note shortly, when the feast days were inaugurated, the events they foreshadowed were "to come"; now some of these events have been fulfilled. Our understanding of the expression "the body is of Christ", noting the context, is that the substance is of Christ, in contrast to the shadow which was associated with the Law.

It is well worth considering these feast days, the new moon, and the sabbath days in more detail. The key chapters for information on the feast days are Leviticus 23 (describing the time *when*), Numbers 28-29 (describing the manner *how*), and Deuteronomy 16 (describing the place *where*). The Feasts of Jehovah came in two basic varieties: one-day feasts (Passover, Firstfruits, Pentecost, Trumpets, Atonement) or seven-day feasts (Unleavened Bread, Tabernacles). The distinction is this: one-day feasts foreshadow once-for-all historical events; the seven-day feasts foreshadow periods of time. We have no doubt as to the event foreshadowed in the Passover; this is made clear in 1 Corinthians 5.7: "even Christ our passover is sacrificed for us". We do not remember the death of Christ on the 14th day of the first month annually; rather, we show forth the Lord's death on a weekly basis in the Lord's Supper (Acts 20.7; 1 Cor 11.23-26), and it should be in our minds daily. Some readers may have in mind Paul's words in 1 Corinthians 5.8: "Therefore let us keep the feast, not with old leaven, neither with the leaven of malice and wickedness; but with the unleavened bread of sincerity and truth". There is no conflict with Paul's teaching here in Colossians 2.16. The feast to be kept is the Feast of Unleavened Bread, the seven-day feast which followed the Passover. It is clear that Paul did not intend for the Corinthians to keep this feast just for seven days! Neither did he mean them to eat literal unleavened bread, as the above quotation makes clear. Rather, this seven-day feast was to characterise the whole of the life of the believer, as the moral consequence of benefiting from the sacrifice of Christ as the true Passover lamb. The Feast of Firstfruits foreshadowed the resurrection of Christ (1 Cor 15.20, 23); again, we are not to commemorate this just on one day of the year! The Day of Pentecost was fulfilled with the descent of the Holy Spirit (Acts 2.1). The final three feasts, which were placed in the autumn of Israel's calendar, are still future. On the first day of the seventh month was the Feast of Trumpets. This anticipates the regathering of Israel (see Isaiah 27.12-13 and Matthew 24.31). While some have applied this to the trumpet at the Lord's return to the air (1 Thess 4.16; 1 Cor 15.52), the true interpretation of the feast is certainly connected to Israel's national regathering. Even allowing for an application to us today, we should not be considering the Lord's return just on the first day of the seventh month. The Day of Atonement took place on the tenth day of the seventh month. This foreshadows the repentance of Israel upon the return of their Messiah. Isaiah 53 and Zechariah 12.10-14 are key Scriptures in this regard, for example, when "they shall look upon me whom they have pierced, and shall mourn for him, as one mourneth for his only son" (Zech 12.10). Finally, there was the seven-day Feast of Tabernacles, which foreshadows the coming Kingdom of the Lord Jesus for 1,000 years. Peter caught the significance of this upon the "holy mount" (2 Pet 1.18; Mt 17.4). The Lord had said in Matthew 16.28, "there be some standing here, which shall not taste of death, till they see the Son of man coming in his kingdom". These words were fulfilled days later, when Peter, James and John got a foretaste of His kingly glory. Peter's response was to suggest the building of tabernacles – he clearly linked his experience to the Feast of Tabernacles.

What, then, should our attitude be to these feasts? We should certainly study them, not to keep them as a matter of ritual, but to rejoice in the unfolding of events in God's calendar, some of which are fulfilled, while the final three remain future as we write. In Numbers 28.11-15, we find details of the sacrifices to be offered "in the beginning of your months". This seems to be the link to the reference to "new moon" in Colossians 2.16. The cycle of the new moon is this: emergence from darkness to the zenith of the full moon, then the decline back to darkness. This seems an apt figure for Israel's history - the emergence from the darkness of Egyptian bondage to the full moon of the kingdom in the days of David and Solomon, then the decline to darkness in the captivities at the hands of the Assyrians and Babylonians. Israel has never recovered the days of David and Solomon's reigns – and will only do so during the glorious reign of Christ. Each month, Israel collectively was to offer two young bullocks, one ram, seven lambs for a burnt offering and one kid for a sin offering, along with associated meat and drink offerings. We are not called to this! Our need for renewal has been fully met in the death, resurrection and present life of Christ.

Finally, Paul mentions "sabbath days" (the best texts omit the definite article) or, as the plural word could be translated, 'weeks'. The sabbath was introduced by God after completing the work of creation. God "rested on the seventh day from all his work which he had made" (Gen 2.2). That the entrance of sin disturbed this rest is equally clear; in Genesis 3.21 the Lord God is working again, this time in the provision of a covering of skin for Adam and Eve. This working has not ceased. When persecuted by the Jews for performing a sign on the sabbath, the Son of God said, "My Father worketh hitherto, and I work" (Jn 5.17). How could the Son rest on the sabbath if the Father was working? The Father continues to work, as Paul reminds the Philippians: "He which hath begun a good work in you will perform it until the day of Jesus Christ" (Phil 1.6) and, again, "it is God which worketh in you both to will and to do of his good pleasure" (2.13). This work is not restricted to six days of the week; God continues to work in His people, and this continues daily.

Jewish Mysticism (2.18-19)

In these two verses we will find seven matters brought together in Paul's argument, namely:

- Loss of reward (2.18)
- Misplaced worship (2.18)
- Embrace of speculation (2.18)
- Flesh promoted (2.18)
- Headship abandoned (2.19)
- Spiritual resources rejected (2.19)
- Divine increase denied (2.19)

The verses begin with a warning: "Let no man beguile you of your reward" (v 18). To be 'beguiled' in the manner Paul has in mind will impact the believer's reward, both future and present. The stakes are indeed high! To appreciate the nature of the possible deception, we need to briefly reflect on the claims of Gnostic sects. Gnostics postulated a vast gulf between the supreme God and the lower material world, a gulf occupied by hierarchies of spirit beings, such as angels. They claimed to have access to these beings and, through this, to have attained a higher knowledge. These claims, of course, are in direct contradiction to the Gospel, which shows us how we can have a relationship with God as His sons and be brought into union with Christ, being indwelt by the Spirit of God.

The first aspect of life impacted by adopting the Gnostic teaching was worship - worshipping angels rather than God. The humility mentioned here was really a false humility: it was argued that, because God is far above us, it was appropriate, indeed spiritual, to worship beings less than God. This flatly contradicted the revelation of Scripture. God is indeed immeasurably greater than us, but the divine command remains: "Thou shalt worship the Lord thy God, and him only shalt thou serve" (Mt 4.10). Indeed, the Lord Himself revealed that true worshippers "worship the Father in spirit and in truth: for the Father seeketh such to worship him" (Jn 4.23). Furthermore, when John was about to worship an angel, he was rebuked with the words, "See thou do it not: for I am thy fellowservant, and of thy brethren the prophets, and of them which keep the sayings of this book: worship God" (Rev 22.9). The instruction could not be clearer: worship God. We can draw this important practical lesson: any teaching which compromises our worship of God should be rejected, no matter the appealing nature of the arguments presented to justify it. The error here arose because what God had revealed had not been believed.

Rejecting the revelation of God in Scripture opens the mind to the mere speculation of men. This is the import of the expression, "intruding into those things which he hath not seen" (Col 2.18). The Gnostic falsely claimed to be initiated into a sphere which, actually, he had not seen. This was simply self-deception. The Colossians were faced with the choice of divine revelation against the empty speculation of men. How did these men know about this unseen world? It was not by divine revelation; Paul categorises this speculation as the empty product of a proud, fleshly mind. The supposed humility of the adherents was but a cloak for excessive pride. The phrase 'proud to be humble' captures the spirit of these false teachers. They took pride in their supposed spirituality and higher knowledge; however, it was, in fact, the operation of the flesh - man's fallen sinful nature. Gnosticism can be regarded as a knowledge religion, not based on divine grace to unworthy sinners, but the special insight of the initiated adherents, coupled with an ascetic lifestyle.

The dangers to the Colossians of this teaching are further explored in verse 19: to accept this teaching would mean "not holding the Head". This is nothing less than abandoning the headship of Christ over His Body, the Church. The term "the Head" is to be regarded as a title of the Lord Jesus, presenting him as the Head of the Church which is His Body. This involves the vital union of each believer with Christ, and presents to us the Church as the Body of Christ. This union does not require the intervention or action of any angelic or other spirit being; it is a union with a divine Person, the Lord Jesus Christ, in Heaven. Holding the Head is the action of faith, holding fast to Christ as our exalted Head.

This union of the Church with Christ provides us with an inexhaustible supply of spiritual provision to meet our needs and produce growth and advancement. The believer does not need to look beyond Christ; He is all-sufficient. The thought of spiritual provision is contained in the phrase, "by joints and bands having nourishment ministered, and knit together". In a physical body, the "joints" are ligaments, possibly referring to the nerves[18] or the joints of contact between the members of the body. The "bands" have the function of binding together. The parallel passage in Ephesians 4.16 is important to note: "From whom the whole body fitly joined together and compacted by that which every joint supplieth, according to the effectual working in the measure of every part, maketh increase of the body unto the edifying of itself in love". The quotation from Ephesians suggests that the joints are joints of supply. In the context, this refers to the gifts given to the Church whereby the saints can be edified. In Colossians 2.19, "having nourishment ministered" has the thought of being supplied, not physically, but spiritually. Union with Christ our Head opens up to us a constant source of spiritual nourishment requisite for our spiritual advancement. Thus, the "joints" are connected with supply, and "bands" are connected with being "knit together". A band, in this context, is that which is known in the body as uniting the members together. Perhaps Ephesians 4.4-5 succinctly expresses this: "one body, and one Spirit, even as ye are called in one hope of your calling; one Lord, one faith, one baptism, one God and Father of all". To heed the false claims of the Gnostics was to abandon this source of spiritual nourishment and the unity of the one Body. Devastating indeed were the consequences of embracing this false teaching.

The final consequence presented here of the union of Christ and the Church is the idea of increase: "increaseth with the increase of God" (Col 2.19). Presumably, the appeal of the Gnostic teaching to some was that it offered a route to spiritual advancement. This turns out to be illusory, because the actual route to spiritual advancement is the enjoyment of union with Christ our Head, in the context of the Body of Christ. We need the ministry of other believers to assist us in our spiritual growth and development. Without even understanding precisely what Paul means by the "increase of God", we can at least see that it follows from holding fast to the Head. A vital faith in Christ, acknowledging Him as the sole Head of the Body, is therefore necessary for growth. Benefiting from what He supplies, doubtless through other members of the Body, leads to increase. This increase is not to be viewed in terms of new converts but, rather, in the spiritual development of existing believers. The phrase, "the increase of God", may be viewed in a number of ways. It would certainly include the thought of increase which is from God – with God as its source. After all, Paul taught the Corinthians that "God … giveth the increase" (1 Cor 3.7). Perhaps, too, it is increase which is the result of God working. In Philippians 1.6, we learn that God has "begun a good work in you" and, again, "it is God which worketh in you" (2.13). This divine work is to result in increase, which we could classify as divinely sourced and produced.

The reader may be forming the view that this teaching is of little interest to us because we simply would not be deceived by the sort of ideas propagated by the Gnostics. Even if this be so, there are, nonetheless, some important practical applications to note. Firstly, while it is appropriate to have a deep sense of our own personal unworthiness, which should produce humility of mind (Col 3.12), this should be mixed with faith in the statements of Scripture which show us the honour God has conferred upon us in Christ and as His sons. We need to avoid the trap of taking pride in supposedly being humble. Secondly, anything which compromises our worship of God is to be rejected. Thirdly, Christ as our Head is all-sufficient. We need look to no other source for supply to produce spiritual advancement. Fourthly, we need to look for increase, not effected by our own wisdom, but that which is of God. This applies both to Gospel work and to the teaching of the saints. Christ has made provision for the ongoing advancement of the saints; it is our business to hold fast to Him.

We conclude by returning to the thought of loss of reward. The teaching of the Gnostic would rob the true believer of the enjoyment of being a member of the Body of Christ, united to Christ our Head. That said, to fully follow the Gnostic philosophy would be to abandon the Scripturally-revealed Christ altogether, and to leave the worship of the Creator for the worship of the creature, albeit angels. This is eternally ruinous for any soul, and simply reflects the falseness of the original profession. As John the apostle later wrote, "they went out from us, but they were not of us" (1 Jn 2.19).

Chapter 8

Preservation from Asceticism (2.20 – 3.4)

This section deals with two matters:

- The Futility of Asceticism (2.20-23)
- The Secret Life of the Believer (3.1-4)

Wherefore if ye be dead with Christ from the rudiments of the world, why, as though living in the world, are ye subject to ordinances, (Touch not; taste not; handle not; which all are to perish with the using); after the commandments and doctrines of men? Which things have indeed a shew of wisdom in will worship, and humility, and neglecting of the body; not in any honour to the satisfying of the flesh. If ye then be risen with Christ, seek those things which are above, where Christ sitteth on the right hand of God. Set your affection on things above, not on things on the earth. For ye are dead, and your life is hid with Christ in God. When Christ, who is our life, shall appear, then shall ye also appear with him in glory (Col 2.20 – 3.4).

The Futility of Asceticism (2.20-23)

In the closing verses of chapter 2, Paul identifies the ineffectiveness of the stringent asceticism advocated by those following Gnostic teaching. Such claimed that this was the way to distance oneself from the lower material world and to gain access to spiritual insight and advanced knowledge. Paul's conclusion is that such man-made programmes and edicts are "not of any value against the indulgence of the flesh" (2.23, RV). We need to be clear on this point: Paul was certainly not advocating, or even permitting, a life of indulgence on the part of the believer, as chapter 3 makes abundantly clear. Indeed, the Lord Himself taught His disciples that "if any man will come after me, let him deny himself, and take up his cross, and follow me" (Mt 6.24). Rather, Paul was showing that the ascetic practice advocated by the Gnostics as a condition for advancement was ineffective. A key statement to note is that the practices advocated by the Gnostic were "after the commandments and doctrines of men" (Col 2.22). This was a humanly-devised approach, not one commanded by God through the revelation of Scripture.

Paul's approach to dealing with this element of Gnostic error can be identified as follows:

- *A Statement of Doctrine:* "If ye be dead with Christ ..." (2.20)
- *A Question:* "Why, as though living in the world, are ye subject to ordinances?" (2.20)
- *A Conclusion:* "Which things have indeed ..." (2.23)

In his conclusion, Paul identifies two matters of importance:

- *The Appearance of the Ascetic Life:* "Which things have indeed a shew ..." (2.23)
- *The Reality of the Ascetic Life:* "Not of any value against the indulgence of the flesh" (2.23, RV)

Paul begins with a statement of doctrine, reminding the Colossians of what was true of them in association with Christ: "Wherefore if ye be dead with Christ from the rudiments of the world" (v 20). The word "wherefore" has a similar import to 'therefore', insofar as it prompts us to reflect on what has gone before, notably in verse 12, where, in their baptism, the believers bore witness to the fact they had died with Christ. The "if" is not the 'if' of doubt but, rather, the 'if' of argument. Paul is saying, 'since' you died with Christ then why follow this man-made scheme of denial? A particular aspect of our being "dead with Christ" is presented here; we are to understand that we are "dead with Christ to the rudiments of the world". The word "rudiments" carries the idea of 'elements' (JND) or first things and, in the context, takes the sense of rudimentary religious principles. In verses 3 and 9 of Galatians chapter 4, it is used of the "weak and beggarly" elements of Judaism. Far from being advanced, Gnosticism was elementary - it relied on the elementary ideas of human effort and wisdom. The origins of this can be found in Genesis 3: the first thought of Adam and Eve was to provide a covering for themselves, devised and produced by themselves, which proved totally ineffective. When God moved into the garden, they sought to hide themselves among the trees. Adam confessed, "I heard thy voice in the garden, and I was afraid, because I was naked" (Gen 3.10), even though he was wearing an apron of fig leaves. The association of the believer with Christ in His death has separated us from these elementary principles.

On this doctrinal foundation, Paul poses a question: "Why, as though living in the world, are ye subject to ordinances … after the commandments and doctrines of men?" (Col 2.20, 22). We will shortly deal with the explanatory parenthesis: "Touch not; taste not; handle not" (v 21). Paul challenges those attracted to the ascetic life to recognise that it was of human construction; its origin was in the teaching of men and carried only man's authority. Paul, in effect, asks, why are you subjecting yourselves to the authoritative decrees of men? The cornerstone for the believer's advancement is the acknowledgement of what is true of us in association with Christ, in His death and resurrection. We bow to the authority of the Lord, and are directed by the revelation of Scripture; the doctrines and commandments of men play no part. Indeed, we will find that these lead us into conflict with Scripture. Recall the challenging question from the Lord to the Pharisees: "Why do ye also transgress the commandment of God by your tradition?" (Mt 15.3).

The explanatory parenthesis captures the essence of the ascetic lifestyle: it focused on sensory denial, though, interestingly, Paul does not say, 'look not' or 'hear not'. The word "touch" means to handle, and it is used variously in the New Testament. In John 20.17, the Lord used the word when addressing Mary - "Touch me not" - indicating that she was not to cling to Him so as to retain Him here on Earth. In 1 Corinthians 7.1 - "It is good for a man not to touch a woman" - the word is used of sexual relations. The word "taste" carries the idea of partaking, and also possibly of enjoying, whereas "handle not" refers to even a light or fleeting touch. These terms convey the punctilious efforts of the adherent to deny even the most innocent and needful interaction with the world with their senses, as a means of supposedly advancing to a state of spiritual insight and knowledge. Such was, in fact, a delusion. The phrase, "which all are to perish with the using" (Col 2.22), qualifies the preceding list to items that are consumable and can be used up. There is a fundamental flaw in the thinking behind this scheme of self-denial; denying sensory interaction with the material world, which incidentally we cannot avoid, does not imply a condition and ability to gain a higher spiritual insight or state. This teaching fails to appreciate the strength of man's fallen nature and man's want of strength to effect any spiritual advancement. Man's problem is with his heart, as the Lord taught: "For out of the heart proceed evil thoughts, murders, adulteries, fornications, thefts, false witness, blasphemies" (Mt 15.19). Man needs Christ and the power of the indwelling Holy Spirit. A man can shut in the body, but he cannot do the same as easily with the thoughts.

In his conclusion, Paul acknowledges how the ascetic life may appear: "which ... have ... a shew of wisdom in will worship, and humility, and neglecting of the body" (Col 2.23). There might be "a shew of wisdom" in this programme of self-denial, but it was not divine wisdom - it was but an expression of human wisdom. The idea of "will worship" is of voluntarily adopted worship (JND), not that which is imposed by others. The adherents of this system viewed themselves as free from mere formal acts of worship, and had committed themselves to voluntary worship. Sadly, noble as this aim was, it did not lead to them to be "true worshippers" who worshipped the Father "in spirit and in truth" (Jn 4.23). There was no doubt either that, in the eyes of the adherents, they had humbled themselves in denying the material world. This again proved to be illusory, since they had not humbled themselves before God as sinners in need of forgiveness. As already noted, this supposed humility turned out to be a cloak for pride, with speculations "vainly puffed up" (Col 2.18) in their fleshly mind. There was also no doubt that they had gone in for "neglecting of the body" (v 23). They subjected themselves to a regime of unsparing severity and harsh treatment of the body, but was it effective?

Paul had no doubt about the answer. The rendering in the *Revised Version* makes the sense plain: asceticism was "not of any value against the indulgence of the flesh". Paul will show how the sins of the flesh are to be dealt with in the next chapter (3.5-8), but here he shows that the best efforts of undoubtedly sincere individuals were ineffective. The reason is important to re-state: man's failing starts in the heart, not with the material world. Man's fallen nature leads him to abuse the provision of the material world and to abuse the senses which God has given him, but the issue is internal, not external. The answer is not in self-effort, but in the death and resurrection of Christ. This Paul continues to develop in chapter 3.

In summary, in chapter 2, Paul has provided an answer to the erroneous claims of Gnosticism, while, at the same time, stressing the union and association of the believer with Christ, our exalted Head. We have no reason to look to another - Christ is all-sufficient for the saint in his or her desire for spiritual advancement. This is also the doctrinal basis for the very practical teaching we find in the balance of the epistle. Paul begins by setting out the practical implications of our union and association with Christ in Heaven, and we will see that this impacts our goals in living, our character, and our relationships. The opening verses of chapter 3 are then the counterpart of his warning about asceticism, and we have coupled it in our discussion of asceticism for that reason. While the believer is involved with everyday family, business and assembly life, each believer must have a secret life. This is the subject matter of the next four verses.

The Secret Life of the Believer (3.1-4)

The heading for this section is drawn from the words of Colossians 3.3: "for ... your life is hid with Christ in God". The word "hid" is translated "secret" in Matthew 13.35. This clearly does not imply a monastic existence, separated from other human beings and family, as the balance of this chapter makes clear. It does imply that each believer should have a secret life with God, the nature of which we now explore.

The content of the opening four verses of chapter 3 can be summarised as follows:

- The Believer's Desire (3.1)
- The Believer's Occupation (3.2)
- The Believer's Life (3.3)
- The Believer's Prospect (3.4)

The structure of these opening four verses is also straightforward to observe. We have:

- *The Basis for Paul's Exhortation:* "If ye then be risen with Christ" (3.1)
- *Two Exhortations:* "Seek" (3.1) and "set your affection" (3.2)
- *A Supporting Reason:* "For ye are dead" (3.3)
- *A Glorious Prospect:* "When Christ ... shall appear, then shall ye also appear with him in glory" (3.4)

The chapter begins with an "if". Again, this is not the 'if' of doubt, but of argument; Paul is saying, since it is true that you are risen with Christ, then it follows that you should seek those things which are above. Our first task is to understand how Paul's exhortation follows from this statement of doctrine. We have already seen that Paul has spoken extensively of the association of the believer with Christ, for example, "quickened together with [Christ]" (2.13), and "dead with Christ from the rudiments of the world" (v 20). Here, in chapter 3 verse 1, we are associated with Christ in His resurrection. It is important to see the connections between these statements. That we have been "quickened together with him" (2.13) is God's answer to the fact that we were, in pre-conversion days, "dead in [our] sins and the uncircumcision of [our] flesh" (v 13). That we are "risen with Christ" (3.1) is the answer to the fact that we are "dead with Christ from the rudiments of the world" (2.20). What happened when Christ rose? Amongst other important matters, Christ bodily left the tomb, the realm or place of death, to live in a resurrection sphere, presently at the right hand of God. What is the implication of our association with Christ in this event? We are to recognise that our life is no longer in the place of death (the sphere where the rudiments of the world pertain) but, as being bound to Christ, our life is now connected to where He is. This is the thrust of the apostle's exhortation. We are to "seek" things which are above. This is a statement about our desires, which impacts our will and heart. In blunt terms, what do we want? Paul says, you will want things above. The nature of the "things which are above" is now identified by three important phrases in verse 1 of chapter 3:

- "Where Christ"
- "Sitteth"
- "On the right hand of God"

The false teachers of chapter 2 might have claimed to be seeking things above, but their vision was far below what we have here. The believer desires things which pertain to the Man who is presently seated on the right hand of God. This surpasses, by far, anything the Gnostic could offer. The present desires of the saint are to be fixed on the place where Christ is now. This is an aspect of truth missed by many: the present life and ministry of Christ in Heaven. Just as we are often amazed at the wealth of activity the Lord engaged in while on Earth, the New Testament epistles, in particular, reveal the vast range of what our Lord is now doing in Heaven. Take, for the sake of illustration, the Epistle to the Hebrews: we find some different aspect of the present life and ministry of Christ in almost every chapter. A more detailed consideration of this is left to the reader to pursue. For each saint, it is important to learn about the Lord when He was here; the Gospels provide a ready source of precious truth on this front. However, it is equally important for us to know details of His present life and ministry, where Christ is presently in Heaven. Paul notes for us that Christ is "sitting" (JND). This is an important detail which conveys a number of truths. That Christ is sitting is connected with the fact that the work of sacrifice is forever complete (Heb 10.12). This is equally true in the Colossian epistle, where redemption has been secured (1.14), peace has been made (v 20), and reconciliation has been effected (vv 21-22), not forgetting the victory over wicked principalities and powers (2.15). The seated Christ reminds us of the wide-ranging triumph of His suffering and sacrifice.

There is more, though. The Gospel writers detail occasions when our Lord is viewed as being seated. For instance, in Luke 4.20, He sat to give the sense of the Scripture He had just read in the synagogue in Nazareth and, in Luke 5.3, He was seated in Simon's boat to teach the multitude. Later, in Luke 22.14, He sat down with the 12 apostles for fellowship and, in resurrection, we find Him sitting at meat in the house of Cleopas (24.30). These simple observations are illuminating. The seated Christ is connected with Him teaching, and the enjoyment of fellowship with Him. Though now in Heaven, our Lord still delights in the same. He is most definitely the source of spiritual nourishment for the body (Col 2.19); after all, we have learned that in Him are "hid all the treasures of wisdom and knowledge" (v 3). Later, in chapter 3 verse 16, we will consider the apostolic exhortation, "Let the word of Christ dwell in you richly". This is the word which comes from the seated Christ at the right hand of God. It is the word which comes from the exalted Head of the Body through the Scriptures, and which is ministered through His servants. The second thought is that of fellowship. Just as the Lord wanted to have the fellowship of His disciples on Earth, so too now that He is seated in Heaven. These are things we are to desire.

The final key matter is where Christ is seated: "on the right hand of God" (3.1). That He is so seated is indicative of His personal divine right – this is His rightful place (Heb 1.3), of His Father's approval – He sits there by His Father's invitation (v 13), and of His unrivalled supremacy – He is far above all principality and power and might and dominion (Eph 1.20-21). He is, by reason of the place where He sits, the One with supreme power and blessing. He far exceeds any angelic being or the mightiest principality and power. The Gnostics thought no higher than what they considered to be intermediary created beings. The believer in Christ desires things connected with the very Creator of all things, the seated Christ on the right hand of God. Our life, as risen with Christ, is now in the sphere where He is.

There is a final thought regarding His being seated. It is the repose of One at peace. In Colossians 3.15 (JND), Paul again exhorts the Colossians to "let the peace of Christ" rule in their hearts; this is the peace which is sourced in the seated Christ on the right hand of God. There is no disturbance on the right hand of God; it is a place of undisturbed peace. Since He is seated there, we can have His peace in our hearts now. May this thought comfort the troubled and anxious.

In verse 2, Paul exhorts the believers to "set your affection on things above, not on things on the earth". The idea is to 'mind' things above; this has to do with our mental occupation - we are to turn our mind to things above, then think upon and contemplate them. This involves the moral interest and reflection of the believer. These words have evoked the sceptical comment, 'too heavenly-minded to be of any earthly use'. This is demonstrably false; take, for instance, our Lord Himself. He was in constant communion with His Father in Heaven and accomplished more on Earth than any other in history. We could also cite the Apostle Paul as an example of a heavenly-minded man. The truth is, rather, that we will be of no earthly use if we are not heavenly-minded. Our problem today is not that we are too heavenly-minded, but that we are too earthly-minded! The beautiful and practical life described in this chapter and the next flows from minding "things above". The apparently vague term, "things above", is used to encompass all that is open to us by revelation, connected with Christ now at the right hand of God. It includes the vast scope of the present life and ministry of Christ. We would do well to reflect individually on the amount of time in any day or week that we spend positively minding "things above". Evidently, there are matters of life on Earth that need a place in our thinking, but the challenge comes to assess to what degree we are prepared to allocate time getting to know the present life of Christ in Heaven - to engage with things above.

The positive exhortation is reinforced by the negative: "not on things on the earth". What "things" does the apostle have in mind? Certainly, this includes those earthly things mentioned by the apostle in chapter 2, including philosophy originating in the tradition of men (v 8), the shadows contained in Jewish ritual and type (vv 16-17), the mystical speculations regarding angels (v 18) and, finally, the ineffective approach of asceticism (vv 22-23). These are all earthly things. We could add to this list many other temporal aspects of life on Earth that simply distract from the enjoyment of eternal life. Verse 3 of chapter 3 provides the reason that justifies the apostolic exhortation: "For ye are dead, and your life is hid with Christ in God". Evidently, there are two parts to this reason, both relating to what is now true of every believer. Firstly, "ye are dead". This must be understood in the context, notably, chapter 2 verse 20, where we learned that the believer is "dead with Christ from the rudiments of the world". As we have previously noted, death brings separation and, in this context, a separation from the "rudiments of the world". If we have died to these earthly things we cannot go on living in them, and they are not to dominate our thinking.

Positively, our "life is hid with Christ in God". This statement is based on two doctrinal facts, specifically, we have been "quickened together with him" (2.13), and we are "risen with [Him]" (3.1). There are two immediate implications: firstly, we are alive with Christ; secondly, this life is focused on where Christ now is. Although not the central thought in the context, it is appropriate to note that these words certainly imply the security of the believer. Our life is hid with Christ *in God*; there is no safer place! The Lord spoke about the security of His sheep: "neither shall any man pluck them out of my hand" (Jn 10.28), and "no man is able to pluck them out of my Father's hand" (v 29). It is also appropriate to consider the idea that our life is "hid". Why so? Simply because the Lord Himself is presently hid from the eyes of the world. Paul will draw out the contrast in the following verse by referring to the appearing of the Christ in the future. The world has no sense of the present life of Christ in Heaven, even if they accept the truth of His resurrection. Christ to them is hidden, out of sight, and mostly out of mind. For the believer, minding things that now pertain to a living Christ in Glory, that life is also hid; the world neither knows nor cares for it. This is the secret life of communion of the believer with divine Persons; a life the world knows nothing of. The expression "in God" confirms that our life here is immersed in God and in His things.

Lest there be any misunderstanding, let us note that the fruit of this life is certainly seen on Earth. Although Christ is hidden, the purpose of His Body on Earth is to manifest the Head. Individually, the character of Christ is to become the character of the saint, which Paul details throughout this chapter.

We now come to the glorious prospect before the believer as detailed in verse 4: "When Christ, who is our life, shall appear, then shall ye also appear with him in glory". Paul looks forward to the appearing of the Lord Jesus Christ. In this regard, it is assuring to note that he begins with "when", not 'if'. The future appearing is a certainty in the purpose of God. We know from other Scriptures that this event will be after the Lord's coming to the air to take us to the Father's house (1 Thess 1.10; 4.13-18; Jn 14.2-3), and after the days of tribulation and great tribulation (Mt 24.29-30). The precise day and hour of His appearing is in the Father's power (v 36). The description of the Lord here is important to note: "Christ our life". In verse 3, we considered "your life is hid with Christ"; now there is an advance in thought - "Christ" has now become "our life". This will be true for every saint on the occasion of His appearing. Our life, freed from earthly care and occupation, will be absorbed and totally focused on and with Christ: He is our life. There is a present challenge in this regard. In Philippians 1.21, Paul was able to say, "to me to live is Christ". He had arrived in his soul at the evaluation, "I count all things but loss for the excellency of the knowledge of Christ Jesus my Lord" (3.8), and his desire was simply "that I may know him" (v 10). For Paul, his life even while here on Earth was Christ. This can be ours too, but it will only be so in the measure we mind things above, where Christ is.

As already noted, Paul was looking forward to "when Christ, who is our life, shall appear". The idea in the word "appear" is that of being manifested. The contrast is clear: now Christ is hidden from the eyes of the world; then He will be seen. Scripture details this wonderful occasion in Revelation 1.7: "Behold, he cometh with clouds; and every eye shall see him". His manifestation will be universally witnessed by men on Earth. The Lord spoke about this great event in Matthew 24.30: "then shall all the tribes of the earth mourn, and they shall see the Son of man coming in the clouds of heaven with power and great glory". It is on this occasion that He will deal with the Man of Sin, the Wicked One, "whom the Lord shall consume with the spirit of his mouth, and shall destroy with the brightness of his coming" (2 Thess 2.8). The details of His manifestation are further described in Revelation 19.11-16. This is the great day of vindication for our Lord Jesus. The last time this world saw Him, He was hanging on a shameful cross; the next time it will be as the undisputed "KING OF KINGS, AND LORD OF LORDS" (Rev 19.16). We should certainly be amongst those who "love his appearing" (2 Tim 4.8), not least because this revelation has been given to Him by God the Father (Rev 1.1).

Wonderfully, on that great day for the Lord, He will have His Church associated with Him: "then shall ye also appear with him in glory" (Col 3.4). Presently, our life is hid; then, we will be manifested with Christ. The world will then see the saints in a new light; they will be seen sharing the glory of Christ and participating in His rule of the Millennial Earth (1 Cor 6.1-3). It would seem that the Son of God had this in mind when He said, "the glory which thou gavest me I have given them" (Jn 17.22). Again, it will then be that "he shall come to be glorified in his saints, and to be admired in all them that believe" (2 Thess 1.10). All these thoughts should cheer and encourage; it is indeed brighter on before for each saint.

Chapter 9

Putting Off and Putting On (3.5-17)

There is now a marked shift in emphasis in Paul's teaching. Having dealt extensively in chapter 2 with the error facing the Colossian believers, Paul turns his attention to detailing the practical implications of the believer's relationship with Christ. These are both far-reaching and intensely challenging. That said, we need to avoid the trap of disconnecting chapter 3 from what has gone before. There is a sense in which the matters raised in chapters 3 and 4 are a continuation of the apostle's teaching in chapters 1 and 2, and chapter 2 flows into the teaching of chapter 3.

It may be apposite to briefly note the contents of the next part of the epistle, so as to focus our minds on what we are approaching:

- The Old Man and His Deeds (3.5-9)
- The New Man (3.10-11)
- Putting on Christ (3.12-14)
- The Believer's Heart (3.15-17)

Even a cursory glance at these headings reveals the practical nature of the teaching that follows in the final chapters of the letter. There is a simple but important observation: practical teaching rests on the secure foundation of doctrine, and doctrine finds application in practical living. We need both of these aspects of teaching, because the Christian life is not about acquiring theory alone; it must be worked out in our daily lives, otherwise it is of limited value. On the other hand, there is a desire among many believers for practical teaching, but this often translates as practical exhortations with no doctrinal foundation. The result, well-meaning though it may be, is little more than sound-bites and slogans which do not give the saints the power to live them out.

> Mortify therefore your members which are upon the earth; fornication, uncleanness, inordinate affection, evil concupiscence, and covetousness, which is idolatry: for which things' sake the wrath of God cometh on the children of disobedience: in the which ye also walked some time, when ye lived in them. But now ye also put off all these; anger, wrath, malice, blasphemy, filthy communication out of your mouth. Lie not one to another, seeing that ye have put off the old man with his deeds; and have put on the new man, which is renewed in knowledge after the image of him that created him: where there is neither Greek nor Jew, circumcision nor uncircumcision, Barbarian, Scythian, bond nor free: but Christ is all, and in all. Put on therefore, as the elect of God, holy and beloved, bowels of mercies, kindness, humbleness of mind, meekness, longsuffering; forbearing one another, and forgiving one another, if any man have a quarrel against any: even as Christ forgave you, so also do ye. And above all these things put on charity, which is the bond of perfectness. And let the peace of God rule in your hearts, to the which also ye are called in one body; and be ye thankful. Let the word of Christ dwell in you richly in all wisdom; teaching and admonishing one another in psalms and hymns and spiritual songs, singing with grace in your hearts to the Lord (Col 3.5-17).

The Old Man and His Deeds (3.5-9)

The items detailed in verses 5-9 are evidently incompatible with a life of occupation with Christ in Heaven. In this light, Paul gives three weighty instructions to the saints:

- "Mortify therefore your members which are upon the earth" (3.5)
- "Also put off all these" (3.8)
- "Lie not one to another, seeing … ye have put off the old man" (3.9)

"Mortify therefore your members which are upon the earth" (3.5)

There are two specific actions required: "mortify" and "put off". In summary, in verse 5 we find a list of five items to which we are to mortify our members. Verse 6 explains why this action is required: "for which things' sake the wrath of God cometh on the children of disobedience", and verse 7 indicates that, in unconverted days, the Colossian believers, too, lived in these sins. In addition, action is also required to "put off" five further failings (v 8); specifically, lying to each other, because "the old man with his deeds" (v 9) has been put off.

The connection with the preceding verses is supplied by the word "therefore" in verse 5. The matters now covered by Paul are incompatible with, and will rob us of the enjoyment of, the truth of verses 1-4. Additionally, we are to avoid the temptation of compartmentalising our lives into a spiritual part and a part in which we allow ourselves to indulge unhealthy desires. The apostle's teaching relates to our "members which are upon the earth", referring to the limbs of our body. It is through these members that sinful desires find expression. In Matthew 5.29-30, the Lord refers to the eye and the right hand as members, and the tongue is the "little member" mentioned in James 3.5-6. Our body consists of "many members" (Rom 12.4; 1 Cor 12.12) and, doubtless, there is opportunity for the sinful use of many. Elsewhere, Paul exhorts, "Neither yield ye your members as instruments of unrighteousness unto sin: but yield yourselves unto God ... and your members as instruments of righteousness unto God" (Rom 6.13). The righteous use of our members will be described later in Colossians 3 but, presently, the focus is on the need to "mortify" (Col 3.5). The basic idea is to put to death; F F Bruce suggests the sense as "reckon as dead".[19] This indicates that the word has an ethical and mental force, rather than being simply a physical act. We are to reckon that our members are dead to the sinful items about to be described. Here, death brings separation from the sphere and activities in which we once lived, and we are to separate our members from those actions, thoughts and desires which previously characterised our lives. Practically, we are to "make not provision for the flesh, to fulfil the lusts thereof" (Rom 13.14). Readers will be well aware that, amongst other things, this requires the disciplined avoidance of harmful material so readily accessible on the internet.

The first term is "fornication", which refers to illicit sex, sexual activity apart from within marriage,[20] a sin which was both prevalent in the first century and rife in modern society. Along with adultery (that is, intercourse with the spouse of another or intercourse with another who is not one's spouse), fornication is a moral sin that we must avoid. The exhortation of Scripture is pointed and clear: "Flee fornication" (1 Cor 6.18); it is, as Paul explains, a sin against one's own body, a body which belongs to God (v 20). In Ephesians 5.3, it is again the first item in the list of things which are not to be "named among you, as becometh saints". That Paul should find it necessary to so write to the church at Ephesus, as to the assembly at Colosse, makes clear that none of us can afford to be complacent in this matter; the state of mind of reckoning our members dead to fornication needs to be a constant.

The second item is "uncleanness", which is here used in a moral and spiritual sense, referring to all that is inconsistent with God's holiness. Paul reminds the believers in Rome that, in pre-conversion days, they had yielded their members "to uncleanness and to iniquity" (Rom 6.19), but now should yield them to holiness. In 2 Corinthians 12.21, there is a warning to those at Corinth who had "not repented of the uncleanness and fornication and lasciviousness which they have committed". The connection with fornication should be observed. Doubtless, the sin of fornication is preceded by unclean thoughts and desires, and the sin of fornication morally defiles and requires repentance before God. There is no doubt that we live in a world in which there are countless sources of uncleanness; we are to reckon ourselves to be dead to such. Uncleanness, in whatever form, will rob us of the enjoyment of fellowship with divine Persons, and is certainly not consistent with minding things above (Col 3.2).

"Inordinate affection", the third item in our list, is translated "passion" in the *Revised Version*. It relates to a passionate desire,[21] and indicates a drive or force which does not rest until it is satisfied.[22] In 1 Thessalonians 4.5, the word is translated "lust". If one's mind is so consumed by such desires it will rob us of peace and the enjoyment of Christ, and expose the use of our members to sinful acts. In the context, one particular example is the passion that leads to fornication and the associated uncleanness. The next term is "evil concupiscence", meaning evil desires or desires for evil things. The last two terms demonstrate that human desires have been corrupted in two ways: the strength of those desires can become inordinate, and the object of those desires can be evil. Human history bears ample testimony that the previous two desires are never satisfied. This leads on to the following term, "covetousness", which Paul identifies with "idolatry". Covetousness is the desire for more, used always in a bad sense.[23] What men want more of becomes a god to them, so they pursue it with all their heart, and they become a servant to it. The items here portray an individual out of control, giving free rein to their desires, no matter how all-consuming these desires become, or what evil object is desired.

The reason for the exhortation to "mortify" in verse 5 is made clear in verse 6: "for which things' sake the wrath of God cometh on the children of disobedience". God is rightly angry with men and women for the activities and desires listed in the previous verse. It is a clear perversion of the right way. Unsaved individuals are described in verse 6 as "children of disobedience", though it should be noted that "children" should read 'sons'. The point is not so much birth, but character; they are characterised by disobedience to God. This verse clearly shows God's attitude towards unsaved men: He is angry with how they live, yet unconditionally loves them with a view to delivering them from their current manner of life and from the judicial and eternal consequences of their sins. There is a thought held by some, that, because God is a God of love, He sanctions men to live as they please with no consequences. This thinking is folly and self-deception; these Scriptures make clear that "the wrath of God cometh on the children of disobedience". Indeed, even the well-known text of John 3.16 explains that the love of God for the world has in view that we "should not perish".

The Colossians themselves could look back to the period of their lives when they, too, lived in these sins. Looking back to their unconverted days, Paul writes, "in the which ye also walked some time, when ye lived in them" (v 7). This shows the transforming effect of the Gospel in the lives of the Colossian saints. There was a past period of their lives when they walked in the sins of verse 5, but now matters are different. Two terms described their past: "in the which ye also walked", and "ye lived in them". The first points to their manner of life and activity; observing them we would have seen individuals to whom the terms in verse 5 could be aptly applied. Their whole life is said to have been "in them", indicating that life itself consisted for them in pursuing the sins so described. The language of these verses makes clear that this was now in the past for these saints. The exercise of mortifying the members which are on the earth is to ensure that these sins remain firmly in the past, and do not mar the present.

Though consideration of these verses is sobering, it nevertheless shows us the power of the Gospel. The Colossian saints could once be described by the terms of verse 5, but now they were delivered (1.13) and forgiven (v 14), and had been divinely quickened together with Christ (2.13). By virtue of their union and association with Christ, they could desire and set their minds upon a very different world, where Christ is seated on the right hand of God; a world of holiness and righteousness. The same holds for us.

"Also put off all these" (3.8)

In verses 8-9 there are essentially two commands - "put off" and "lie not" - along with the supporting explanation, "seeing that ye have put off the old man with his deeds". Before considering the term "put off", observe that these verses are introduced with the words, "but now ye also". These three words should be noted: "but", "now" and "also". Dealing with the evidently grave matters which require the mortification of our members, the believer might be lax in relation to other failings which require attention. The use of the word "but" alerts us to the need for further action. This action is pressing and immediate, stressed by the word "now"; Paul expects his readers to act with haste to put off the matters about to be described. This is in addition to the need for mortification, hence the use of the word "also".

The basic instruction is for us to "put off". This carries the thought of taking off from oneself, to change one's clothes, to remove one's clothes from oneself.[24] Hence, the action required of the believer is likened to divesting oneself of a garment. The language is consistent with the observation that the particular failings listed are flaws in character which we are not to tolerate in ourselves. The term also emphasises the responsibility we have in addressing these failings; no doubt we need the constant help of the Spirit of God, but here our responsibility is stressed. We are not to pick and choose which to deal with; we are to "put off all these". We shall observe shortly that there is an order to the items listed by the apostle, as often one leads to another.

The first two items listed are "anger" and "wrath" (v 8). "Anger" refers to a settled condition of mind,[25] and frequently has in view the taking of revenge. It is harbouring thoughts and feelings of indignation against another, waiting for the opportunity for expression. It is a more settled state or condition. Allowing such feelings to persist will inevitably lead to actions and words against another, which may well fall within the terms later described by the apostle. In essence, giving way to anger in this context is incompatible with minding things above. In the presence of Christ in Heaven, we find no such feeling of anger expressed. The second word, "wrath", has been described as a burning anger which flares up and burns with the intensity of a fire,[26] and has in mind a more agitated condition of feelings - an outburst of wrath from inward indignation. We might call it a temper. Outbursts of temper are not compatible with the believer minding things above; there are no such outbursts in Heaven. From a practical standpoint, harbouring anger against another consumes the mind, produces a bitter spirit, robs the saint of peace and the enjoyment of Christ, and leads to unworthy thoughts towards other believers. One signature of this is that we spend too much time minding the failings of the saints, and not enough time minding things above. It is not difficult to see that this can readily lead to outbursts when provocation is encountered. That we have been the victim of wrongdoing or slander might well be the case, but this is no justification for anger and wrath; the answer in Colossians 3.13 is forgiveness. If God had acted in the same way toward us, where would we be? These verses highlight an important point: at times we can be guilty of categorising sins according to our perceived sense of seriousness. We are inclined to place those in verse 5 ahead of the items in verse 8. Paul is making clear to us that we cannot tolerate in ourselves the failings of verse 7.

"Malice" has been described as that vicious nature which is bent on doing harm to others.[27] It is the feature of badness, and is the opposite of excellence. It is cited in 1 Corinthians 5.8 as an example of old leaven, and is coupled with wickedness. In a parallel passage in Ephesians 4.31, Paul instructs the believers to put away from them various things, including "all malice". In Titus 3.3, Paul describes the past life of the believer as one of "living in malice". Likewise, Peter says the believer has laid aside "all malice" (1 Pet 2.1). These Scriptures make it abundantly clear that malice is to play no part in the thinking of a believer; it must be put off. Allowing thoughts which wish ill on others leads inevitably, when opportunity presents, to practical expressions of maliciousness. For the believer, malice is completely at variance with the command to "love one another" (Jn 13.34).

The next three items identified by the apostle relate to speech. The connection with what precedes should be clear: anger leading to inward feelings of resentment forms malicious design against another, then finds expression in cruel and untrue words. "Blasphemy", the first of our words, carries the basic idea of defamation or slander. It indicates the attempt to belittle and cause someone to fall into disrepute or bad reputation. It is evil speaking. "Filthy communication" denotes base, dirty, abusive language; it is a far cry from the gracious words which proceeded from the lips of the Lord (Lk 4.22).

"Lie not one to another, seeing … ye have put off the old man" (3.9)

The final exhortation is to "lie not one to another"; truthfulness in what we express in our words is enjoined upon us. How could it be otherwise? Before proceeding, let us consider the development of thought in these verses. The issue starts with inward indignation against another. Harbouring resentment then fuels malice, which finds ultimate expression in denigrating another with falsehoods, with the deliberate purpose of belittling and undermining that individual in the eyes of others, possibly using the basest of language. Filthy communication is commonplace in the world; let it never mark us as believers; it is not the language of Heaven! A sure test of character is how we speak in a crisis; how we respond when wronged, whether we easily lose control of our temper, or harbour grudges awaiting opportunity for revenge. Paul is making clear to us that we cannot afford to tolerate in ourselves such character failing. There is a need "now" to put off these things.

The reason given by the apostle for this action is "that ye have put off the old man with his deeds". Recall that, in verses 45 and 47 of 1 Corinthians chapter 15, reference is made to the "first man". Here, the first man has become the "old man". "Old", in this context, is not used in relation to age, but to the fact that God has finished with this order of man; it has been displaced by the "second man". The "old man" is man in his standing in Adam - a fallen man. The teaching of Romans 6.6 is important to note: "Knowing this, that our old man is crucified with him, that the body of sin might be destroyed, that henceforth we should not serve sin". God has brought this order of man to an end by the cross. He does not seek to improve it; rather, He has judged it in the cross of Christ. A man cannot be accepted before God in his Adam-standing; God will only accept man in Christ. Paul recognised how this applied to himself in Galatians 2.20, when he wrote, "I am crucified with Christ: nevertheless I live; yet not I, but Christ liveth in me". Paul's teaching in the parallel passage in Ephesians 4.22 is illuminating: "That ye put off concerning the former conversation the old man, which is corrupt according to the deceitful lusts". The old man is corrupt, hence the reason God has judged this order of man in the cross. Here, we are reckoned to have "put off" the old man and his deeds. The language carries the idea of stripping off completely. Since the old man has really been put off, we must not, at critical moments, revert to the manner of behaviour which characterised us before conversion. The deeds listed both in verses 5 and 8 are characteristic of the "old man". Since this has been put off, we must not allow the deeds of that old man to mark us now. It is inconsistent with, and a denial of, what we have been made in Christ. In the following verses, the expression of the new man moulds our character and conduct; it is nothing short of putting on Christ. In the sphere of the new, the overriding principle is "Christ is all, and in all" (Col 3.11).

It is important to keep the context of the chapter in mind in our consideration of these verses. The opening appeal of the chapter was to mind things above; blasphemy, evil speaking and lying are utterly inconsistent with this occupation.

The New Man (3.10-11)

Upon conversion, the believer "put on the new man" (v 10), and there is now the additional exhortation to "put on" the characteristic traits of the new man (vv 12-14). This amounts to each believer becoming more like Christ, for "Christ is all, and in all" (v 11). Verses 10-14 amount to the apostle's answer to the basic question: what is the new man like? Paul addresses this question in two ways. In verses 10-11, he indicates the principles associated with the new man; in verses 12-14, the practical characteristics associated with the new man. The reader will have noted the two-fold reference to the expression "put on". In verse 10, it has to do with the *position* of the believer: it is true of every believer in Christ. In verse 11, the *practise* of the believer is in view, with the ongoing conforming of our lives to Christ. Note that the practical teaching of verses 12-14 follows from the principles of verses 10-11, hence the use of "therefore" in verse 12.

Turning now to the details of verses 10-11, observe that Paul identifies four key principles in relation to the new man:

1. *There is ongoing renewal* ("which is renewed" = which is being renewed)
2. *The new man takes character from his Creator* ("after the image of him that created him")
3. *Former distinctions no longer pertain* ("where there is neither …")
4. *The new man is to express Christ* ("Christ is all, and in all")

In considering the first principle, it is important to note that the believer is now a "new man". This newness is a newness in quality; it relates to an individual's spiritual and moral being which finds practical expression in daily living and formation of character. Evidently, it does not imply that the damage to a man's health, for example, incurred by a sinful lifestyle, is immediately rectified. This must await the transformation of the believer's body at the return of the Lord (1 Cor 15.50-58; Phil 3.21). Equally clear is that ceasing from certain forms of sin may well have beneficial effects on one's health, but this is not directly in view in the term "new". Nor does it imply that relationships entered into before conversion are nullified; the marriage relationship, for instance, still stands. With these qualifying comments, note that the word "renewed" involves a continual action[28] by another, in this case God Himself, doubtless through the activity of the Holy Spirit in the life of the believer.

This "new man" is not self-made or man-made; it is created by God, as we have in Ephesians 2.10: "we are his workmanship, created in Christ Jesus unto good works". God's work in the believer is ongoing; this is clear from other passages such as Philippians 2.13 ("it is God which worketh in you") and Philippians 1.6 ("that he which hath begun a good work in you will perform it until the day of Jesus Christ"). The renewal process is with a view to obtaining "knowledge after the image of him that created him" (Col 3.10). The practical renewal comes from the knowledge of God and, in particular, the knowledge of Christ. As we learn of Christ, we are to be conformed into His image. The reader may well recall the very first words spoken about man: "Let us make man in our image, after our likeness" (Gen 1.26). God has not changed His purpose for man; the new man is to be after the image of God. Recall Paul's teaching in Romans 8.29: "For whom he did foreknow, he also did predestinate to be conformed to the image of his Son". What was lost in the first man is realised in the new man.

The third and fourth principles identified by Paul must be held together. The third is that former distinctions no longer apply; the fourth is that, in the new man, "Christ is all, and in all". He is the unifying power. Verse 11 presents a list of eight terms. This seems to be divided into two groups. The first group gives two connected pairs: "neither Greek nor Jew" and "circumcision nor uncircumcision", followed by a list of four terms: Barbarian, Scythian, bond, free. The first pair shows that national distinctions no longer apply. Strictly speaking, then, there is no such thing as a 'Greek' Christian or a 'Jewish' Christian. Furthermore, the man who was a Greek cannot bring anything of what it meant to be 'Greek' to enhance the new man. He might well have been proud of Greek culture, language, learning and government, but this counts for nothing in the sphere where "Christ is all, and in all". Similarly, the Jew might have been proud of temple ritual and ceremonial law, but this is not transferred into the new dispensation. Historically, it has proved disastrous for Christian testimony when facets of Greek philosophy and Jewish ritual became embedded in the Church. The rite of circumcision again no longer pertains; it did not matter if a man had been circumcised or not. As we have seen in Colossians 2.11, in Christ, circumcision is a spiritual concept applying to all believers, not just males. The term 'barbarian' was initially used by Greeks to refer to non-Greeks in relation to their speech, which the Greeks regarded as rude, but the term later came to refer to any foreigner ignorant of Greek language or culture. After the Persian wars, the term acquired a sense of rudeness and brutality. There are two observations to make. On the one hand, no believer should regard a fellow-believer in the way in which the Greek viewed the non-Greek, even if, perhaps, that person lacks education. On the other hand, there is no place for the rudeness in speech or manners which the term 'barbarian' came to epitomise. The Scythians, who were renowned for their violence and savagery, came to be regarded as the lowest of the barbarians. Speaking the truth must not be mistaken for rude dismissal of others, or crude language. These attitudes have no place in the new man; it is not a question of culture, but Christ. Untold damage has been caused by those who supposed that violence was a justifiable means to further the cause of Christ. The history of the Crusades provides tragic examples of brutality and violence perpetrated in the name of Christ, in direct contradiction of this and other Scriptures.

The final pair of terms, "bond nor free", relates to social distinctions which certainly applied at the time of the writing. Many saints were slaves, and some were masters. These distinctions had no place in the assembly. A believer who was a slave was not to feel inferior to a believing master because of their social standing, nor was a master to regard himself as superior. In the sphere of the assembly, they were all brethren. We might apply this to the employee-employer relationship today. Observe that the Gospel did not overturn this prevalent social order, but in the relationship between believers it had no place. In the assembly, social class distinctions must have no bearing on the fellowship and function of the company. Similarly, a "free" man had full rights of citizenship in the Roman Empire, as had Paul (Acts 22.25-28). In the sphere of the things of Christ, this does not confer special status or privilege upon the believer. For every believer, "our conversation [citizenship] is in heaven" (Phil 3.20).

Positively, the new man takes character, spiritually and morally, from Christ - He is "all, and in all". The practical details are developed in verses 12-14, but the principle is stated here. We should not be surprised by this; after all, it is of Christ alone that the Father rent the heavens to declare, "This is my beloved Son, in whom I am well pleased" (Mt 3.17). There is a simple answer to the question, what is the new man like? The new man is the expression of Christ, and Christ alone! This pertains not to a few believers, but is true "in all". The new man is, therefore, not an individual, but an order of manhood, deriving its characteristics from Christ. Each believer is now regarded as being a new man, belonging to this new order of manhood. We will now address the practical implications of these basic principles.

Putting on Christ (3.12-14)

These verses describe the practical traits which are to characterise the believer as a "new man". There are three main matters to note:

1. The three-fold description of the believer (3.12)
2. The seven-fold description of character traits (3.12-13)
3. The over-arching instruction to love (3.14)

Verse 12 begins with the instruction, "put on therefore". We have noted previously that the reference to "put on" in verse 10 occurred at the moment of conversion; the reference here is practical and ongoing. Paul's use of the word "therefore" reminds us that the practical traits described in verses 12-13 follow from the principles identified in verses

10-11. Practical teaching rests on principles, and principles must have practical expression.

Paul gives a three-fold description of the believer in the statement, "as the elect of God, holy and beloved" (v 12). The Colossian saints were, as is every believer, "elect of God". God had chosen them individually before the foundation of the world (Eph 1.4). The pertinent point here is to consider to what God had chosen them. The answer, in the context, is to be like Christ, marked by the seven-fold traits identified in verses 12-13. Additionally, they were "holy and beloved"; the plural is used here so, literally, they were 'holy ones and beloved ones'. The Colossians had been set apart to God and were the objects of His love. Holiness not only requires us to put off the actions of the old man, but also to put on the traits of the new. As beloved of God, God seeks our greatest blessing, which is for us to be like the only perfect Man, Christ. God's purpose that we might be like Christ is the greatest blessing and evidence of His love towards us. In the seven-fold list of verses 12-13, the items relate to our relationship with, and attitudes towards, others, particularly our fellow-believers.

The first item we are to put on is "bowels of mercies" (Col 3.12). These are tender feelings towards others, looking to meet the need of others. In Philippians 1.8, Paul writes, "God is my record, how greatly I long after you all in the bowels [tender mercies] of Jesus Christ". Our Lord was sensitive to the needs of others, and ministered to meet those needs. Paul claims to have those same feelings towards the Philippian saints, and now ministers to meet their spiritual needs. The new man is to be sensitive to the needs of others, with a willingness to help. There is no sense of hardness or indifference in the character of the new man. These tender mercies must have practical expression. This is found in the term "kindness", which is the practical meeting of the needs of others. In Acts 10.38, Peter records of the Lord that He "went about doing good, and healing all that were oppressed of the devil". This is practical kindness. Expressions of kindness, whether material or spiritual, should be a characteristic trait of each believer. How we think about ourselves is an important factor in determining how we interact with others; "humbleness of mind" (Col 3.12) is an attitude of mind where pride is given no place. Of course, the Lord Himself is our great example, as "he humbled himself" (Phil 2.8). As for ourselves, we have no reason to be proud - all we are and have is on account of God's mercy and grace towards us, made good to us because of the sacrifice of the Lord Jesus Christ. Humbleness of mind is that attitude of thinking which accepts all that God has made me in Christ, with no thought of being puffed-up. This state of "humbleness of mind" leads to meekness, the next item mentioned by the apostle.

Meekness is that subjection of our will to the will of God, accepting circumstances which may not be pleasant. Again, our Lord is the supreme example. His exhortation in Matthew 11.29 is well known: "Take my yoke upon you, and learn of me; for I am meek and lowly in heart". Meekness marked the entry of the Lord into Jerusalem: "Behold thy King cometh unto thee, meek, and sitting upon an ass, and a colt the foal of an ass" (21.5). The meekness of Christ is used as the basis of an apostolic appeal: "I Paul myself beseech you by the meekness and gentleness of Christ" (2 Cor 10.1). The new man, faced with difficulties, is to be characterised by a meek spirit. This is to be expressed in "longsuffering" when the saint faces challenging situations. Longsuffering is that patience which bears both injustice and unpleasant circumstances, knowing that all is under the hand of the Lord. In this connection, Paul uses an interesting expression in 2 Thessalonians 3.5: "the Lord direct your hearts into the love of God, and into the patient waiting for Christ". The marginal reading is instructive: "the patient waiting of Christ". Rather than referring to the believer's waiting for the coming of Christ, Paul wants them to show the patience of Christ - the patience He showed when here as He faced the unbelief and opposition of men.

The next item is "forbearing one another", which involves enduring with, or bearing with, another, even though this may be far from our natural reaction. The apostle's use of the expression "one another" suggests he particularly has the relationship between believers in mind. As every reader will recognise, it is all too easy to become irritated by, and impatient with, the failings and inconsistencies of our fellow-brethren and sisters. While it may be true that we have been wronged, slighted, or misrepresented by another believer, the characteristic of the new man in such circumstances is forbearance. This does not mean we become tolerant of sin; it does mean we are prepared to take wrong against ourselves, not to demand our rights, and, in a spirit of meekness, to leave matters to the Lord while showing longsuffering. This is how the Lord conducted Himself while here, and the character of the new man is "Christ is all, and in all" (v 11).

Longsuffering and forbearance are not enough; there must be a willingness to forgive when we have been wronged. Otherwise, we become resentful and even vengeful. Paul recognised that there may be situations when we have "a quarrel against any" (v 13). This is a valid cause for complaint because of the conduct of another towards us, whether that be by deliberate action or by omission. The response of the new man is to forgive. The focus here is not on the repentance of the individual who has wronged us, but on the response of the individual who has been wronged. This is apt; we find it hard to forgive. The standard to be followed is that of Christ: "even as Christ forgave you, so also do ye" (v 13). The parallel passage in Ephesians 4.32 is worth quoting: "forgiving one another, even as God for Christ's sake hath forgiven you". God forgave us on the righteous basis of the shed blood of Christ - Christ had paid for those sins in His suffering for sins (1 Pet 3.18) - and graciously God has forgiven us. Likewise, we are to forgive on the same basis. Put simply, since Christ has forgiven us, and the new man is the manifestation of Christ in us, then we too must forgive.

There is one more key word to follow: "above all these things put on charity, which is the bond of perfectness" (Col 3.14). "These things" refers back to the items mentioned in verses 12 and 13. We might put it this way: charity (love) is to be the overarching principle which will find expression in the various terms we have already considered. For instance, if we love our brethren as we should, we will have "bowels of mercies" toward them, we will seek opportunity to show practical kindness, we will be longsuffering, forbearing and forgiving. Here, love is described as "the bond of perfectness". The word "bond" is a uniting bond. Love is the principle which perfectly unites the actions of verses 12 and 13; they are all the outcome of love - love for Christ and love for our fellow-believers.

The assembly at Colosse, as in any assembly, brought together believers from different backgrounds, with different personalities and temperaments. There was ample opportunity for relationships to fail and the assembly to be divided. God's answer is for each believer to become like Christ now, with the prospect that, in a future day, we will be "conformed to the image of his Son" (Rom 8.29). As we all should know, there will be challenges in our relationships with one another; the key question is how we go about dealing with these situations. Do we manifest Christ is these crisis situations, or do we resort to the tactics and characteristics of the old man? The teaching in this chapter is clear: the old man has been put off and the new man has been put on, so we have an obligation before God to act in the Christ-like way described in Colossians 3.12-14.

The Believer's Heart (3.15-17)

This heading is drawn from the two-fold reference to the believer's heart (vv 15-16). Two important matters are associated with the heart here: peace (v 15) and praise (v 16). As will be readily seen, these Scriptures also present three main exhortations for us to follow, each with reference to our Lord Jesus Christ:

1. "Let the peace of God [Christ, RV, JND] rule in your hearts" (3.15)
2. "Let the word of Christ dwell in you richly" (3.16)
3. "Do all in the name of the Lord Jesus" (3.17)

Observe, too, the two-fold Godward activity which is expected of the believer:

1. "Singing with grace in your hearts to the Lord" (3.16)
2. "Giving thanks to God and the Father by him" (3.17)

Before proceeding, it is important to see that these verses continue the practical teaching of verse 12. This can be observed by noting the use of the word "and" in verses 14, 15 and 17. The teaching we are about to consider flows from, and is required because of, the content of verses 12-14.

Verse 15 contains three clauses, the content of which may be summarised as:

- Our Hearts
- Our Calling
- Our Gratitude

Our Hearts

The first matter to consider is one related to translation. The *Authorised Version* gives "the peace of God"; the *Revised Version* and J N Darby's *New Translation* "the peace of Christ". The "peace of God" is found in Philippians 4.7, which relates to the state of peace which God Himself enjoys; God is at peace. Here, the context supports the alternative rendering, "the peace of Christ". To see this, observe that this section is about the characteristics of the new man, concerning which "Christ is all, and in all" (Col 3.11). Furthermore, in Colossians 2.19, the believer is to be "holding the Head", who is the source of supply of all the body requires. Hence, all comes from the Head, even Christ, so we have the "word of Christ" (3.16), and it seems, therefore, fitting to accept that peace also comes from the Head. Of course, in essence, it is the same peace as in Philippians 4.7 - the peace enjoyed by, and emanating from, deity. This peace is to rule in "your hearts".

This leads to a consideration of what exactly is being referred to here by "your hearts". Reference is not to the physical organ which plays such a vital role in our bodies, but to part of our non-material being. Scripture assigns certain functions or capacities to our heart, some of which may come as a surprise when first encountered. Our capacity to reason is associated with the heart (Gen 6.5; Mk 2.6, 8), as is the exercise of faith (Prov 3.5; Rom 10.9-10). Our heart is also the seat of convictions (Dan 1.8; Acts 11.23) and conscience (1 Sam 24.5; Acts 2.37; 7.54). It is in the sphere of these faculties that peace is required to rule. We tend to associate the heart with emotions, whereas, in Scripture, this is more frequently linked to the soul. To understand further the connection between the heart and peace, it is helpful to reflect on the Lord's own teaching regarding the peace

He gives. Recall John 14.27: "Peace I leave with you, my peace I give unto you: not as the world giveth, give I unto you. Let not your heart be troubled, neither let it be afraid". A heart in which peace does not rule is one open to trouble and fear. Trouble involves agitation and disturbance;[29] the Lord's reference to fear involves fearfulness, cowardice and timidity.[30] How can this arise? The context gives help: in Colossians 3.12-13, we have seen that there are circumstances which arise that require longsuffering, forbearance and a willingness to forgive. The events behind these can easily lead to agitation, and even fear. For example, if we are wronged by a fellow-believer, the resulting agitated state of heart can affect our reasoning, and can lead to distorted judgments and possibly a determination for retribution. However, the peace of Christ dispels both trouble and fear.

The peace of Christ is to "rule" in our hearts. The idea in the word "rule" is to act as an umpire, to arbitrate, and hence to decide. To grasp the import of this, consider the case when peace does not rule. Suppose instead that fear were to rule; then it is not difficult to see that this would impact our faith, our convictions, and even our reasoning. The peace of Christ umpiring the decisions of the heart is necessary for the moral virtues of verses 12 and 13 to be expressed in challenging conditions. A heart devoid of peace, perhaps motivated by revenge, is not likely to be marked by forgiveness. In blessed contrast, the example of our Lord is striking; having just been crucified, He prayed, "Father, forgive them; for they know not what they do" (Lk 23.34).

Before proceeding, we note one final matter. The verse begins with the word "let". There are two things we are to "let": the peace of Christ rule in our hearts, and the Word of Christ dwell in us richly. The word conveys the thought of allowing this to be so. This implies that it lies within us for this to be the case in our lives. If we are to let the Word of Christ dwell in us richly, we have to take positive action: to read, study and believe the Word of Christ. Similarly, we can affect whether or not the peace of Christ rules in our hearts. To appreciate this point, we again need to reflect on some of the terms used by the apostle in verses 12-14. In particular, meekness and humbleness of mind are qualities which result in us submitting to the will of God, possibly in trying circumstances, and not thinking more highly of ourselves than we ought. Pride will stand as a barrier to forbearance and a forgiving spirit which, in turn, is a hindrance to the peace of Christ ruling in our hearts.

Our Calling

The second matter addressed in verse 15 relates to our calling. We are called to this enjoyment of peace in one body - the Body of Christ. This reference to the Body of Christ is to show that the new man is to regulate the conduct of believers with each other. We are called to be members of the Body of Christ. The local assembly in Colosse was the visible manifestation of this (1 Cor 12.27), and it placed believers in contact with those from different backgrounds, with differing temperaments and social standing. How was this going to work in practical terms? Christ intends that we manifest the new man, even when the weakness or failure of fellow-believers makes this challenging. There is a curious inconsistency which at times marks our thinking; we want others to allow for failings in ourselves, but we expect perfection in our brethren. The teaching of this section should allow us to navigate the obvious fact that, although we are now members of one Body, we are not yet perfect. Paul's teaching here shows us how we are to respond to situations when this imperfection manifests itself, possibly to our hurt and loss.

Our Gratitude

The final statement of the verse is "and be ye thankful". At first glance, this does not seem to follow from what has gone before in this verse and the preceding verses. However, a few moments of reflection on the contents of this section (Col 3.10-15) provides plenty of reasons to be thankful. One simple observation is pertinent: peace leads to thanksgiving. The heart enjoying the peace of Christ is lifted to the Father with a deep sense of gratitude. The enjoyment of the peace of Christ is reason enough to give thanks to God; how many in our world today are looking for peace? We have it, both in terms of peace with God (Rom 5.1), but now also with the peace of Christ ruling in our hearts. The second reason in the verse for thanksgiving is connected with our calling. Possibly few of us regularly thank God for such a wonderful calling; we have been called to be part of the Body of Christ. Ours is not to be in the nation of Israel, but in the Body of Christ. Connected with this are the practical opportunities to show what it means to be a new man. When we first trusted in Christ, we ourselves had learned of the dismal failure of the old man, which not only displeased God, but disappointed ourselves. How blessed to have put off the old man and now to have put on the new! This appreciation lifts the heart to God with a deep sense of gratitude.

The content of verses 16-17 can be summarised under the following five headings:

1. The Word of Christ
2. Instruction and Correction
3. Expressions of Praise
4. The Activity of the Believer
5. The Giving of Thanks

1. The Word of Christ

Verse 16 begins with a further exhortation: "Let the word of Christ dwell in you richly". Here, the Word of Christ is the Word of God, viewed from a particular standpoint. We have seen that the believer is a member of the Body of Christ, whose Head, of course, is Christ. In Colossians 2.19, we learned that the Head is the source of supply for the wellbeing of the Body. Hence, here the Word of Christ is the Word that comes to us from the risen Head in Heaven. It is the Word of God, but viewed specifically as coming from Christ our Head. While the Word of God is written and complete, it is also living (Heb 4.12), and Christ uses this written Word to speak to us, to bring to us "a word in season" (Isa 50.4). The exhortation is to allow ("let") this to dwell in us richly. This involves abundance; we are to be rich in the Word of Christ, not impoverished. There is an undoubted richness to the Word of Christ. Even after a lifetime of study of the Scriptures, we are left with the unmistakable sense that there is so much more to discover. There are always further aspects of the "deep things of God" (1 Cor 2.10) to explore. This should thrill our hearts; the Word of Christ is as inexhaustible as the Person from whom it flows. Here is a form of wealth we are to go in for, rather than the transitory material riches of Earth. The wonderful nature of these riches is that they are available to all the saints without limit. Or, rather, any limitation is found in us, not in the Word of Christ.

That we are to "let" the Word of Christ dwell in us richly implies action on our part, as we have noted. We need to give ourselves to the reading of the Scriptures and, Mary-like (Lk 2.19), we need to make time to ponder the Word in our hearts. This takes time and patience – the inescapable truth of Isaiah 28.10 should be noted: "for precept must be upon precept, precept upon precept; line upon line, line upon line; here a little, and there a little". There is no 'quick fix' when it comes to understanding the Word of God. We also need to accept that there are things "hard to be understood" (2 Pet 3.16), but we should cleave to the promise of Scripture: "Consider what I say; and the Lord give thee understanding in all things" (2 Tim 2.7), and the promise of Christ Himself regarding the Holy Spirit: "He will guide you into all truth" (Jn 16.13). That said, Christ our Head does supply spiritual food for us. May our experience be similar to Ezekiel, when the Lord taught him to "eat that I give thee" (Ezek 2.8) and to "eat that thou findest" (3.1). Furthermore, we need to take advantage of opportunities for being taught the Scriptures, as we shall discuss shortly. For the saints at Colosse, this occurred in the assembly gatherings, but also through written teaching such as this very letter from the Apostle Paul, along with the one he wrote to the church at Laodicea (Col 4.16). We must be clear though: Paul had more in mind than simply a knowledge of the Word of Christ. This Word was to "dwell" in them, which involved their acceptance of it by faith – we need to believe the Word of Christ. It was to find a home in their lives, giving them a knowledge and understanding of God, Christ, themselves, their fellow-believers, and the world. It was to frame their worldview, their hope for the future, and their understanding of the past. It was to regulate behaviour, guide decisions, be the substance of their convictions, and provide spiritual nourishment, feeding their hearts and souls while becoming the subject matter for praise.

2. Instruction and Correction

While it is true that each saint has a responsibility to read the Word of God individually, the assembly is to be the sphere where teaching and admonition is given. The instruction is "in all wisdom; teaching and admonishing one another" (3.16). The connection with the Word of Christ should be clear: it is the Word of Christ which becomes the subject matter for teaching and admonition. In this verse, the identity of those teaching is not discussed, only the fact that teaching and admonition needs to be given, that this is based on the Word of Christ, and that "all wisdom" is required in fulfilling this instruction. Firstly, let us consider the matter of teaching. The activity of teaching is aptly summed up in Nehemiah 8.8: "So they read in the book in the law of God distinctly, and gave the sense, and caused them to understand the reading". Reading the Scriptures carefully and with dignity in public gatherings must never be relegated to being a mere precursor to the message to be preached. The Word of God brings its own weight and dignity, and must be read publicly in an appropriately reverent manner. The teacher is then to 'give the sense' of the reading. This clearly involves explaining the truth to the saints in context; in this the teacher strives for simplicity but must avoid being simplistic, which is, in fact, a distortion of the truth. The mark of a gifted teacher is the God-given ability to explain complex and difficult truths in a way in which the saints can understand. Teaching involves more than knowledge and understanding on the part of the teacher – the ability to communicate with clarity is also essential. This does not imply that the delivery of a message becomes an entertaining performance; it does mean that the truth is conveyed clearly in an engaging manner.

In this context, the words of Paul to the Ephesian elders are worthy of note. He reminded them that he had "kept back nothing that was profitable unto you, but have shewed you, and have taught you publickly, and from house to house" (Acts 20.20) and, again, "I have not shunned to declare unto you all the counsel of God" (v 27). Here is the challenge for the teacher and local assembly elders: to what extent is "all the counsel of God" brought to the attention of the saints? Paul was able to say that he kept nothing back from the Ephesians that was to their profit – the response of the saints to this was, and still is, another matter.

There is a second term which goes alongside teaching: admonition. Literally, the word means 'putting in mind',[31] and involves training by word, whether it be encouragement or reproof, and can also involve the giving of a warning. There is evidently a difference between teaching and admonishing. Teaching is principally the imparting of positive truth; admonition is the call to return to right ways when things are wrong, including the issuing of a warning. Both are to be based on the "word of Christ". The order of these terms is important too. Admonition needs the solid base of teaching – there needs to be a ground on which to appeal to the saints which they know and believe. There is a danger that challenging words of admonition have little lasting impact because the reasons for such a course have not been explained to the saints. For example, a word of challenge might be for a newly-converted believer to be baptised, but has anyone taken the time to teach this believer why this is a necessary step? A word of admonition might be given to a young sister for not wearing a head covering to the assembly gatherings, but has she been taught why this is necessary in the first place? Of course, if teaching has been given and is not adhered to, then admonition is most certainly required.

There is also another matter to be considered: "all wisdom" is needed. Knowing what is needed and when is a key insight for the teacher; knowing how to give a word of admonition is another. It is certainly possible to say the right thing in the wrong way. We need to be like our Lord, who knew "how to speak a word in season to him that is weary" (Isa 50.4). While every assembly needs ongoing, systematic Bible teaching, flexibility is also required. Oral ministry must take account of needs as they arise, and reflect the changing spiritual state of both individuals and the assembly as a whole. The wise teacher will be open to the leading of the Spirit, waiting upon the Lord for a message for the saints. After all, Christ our Head knows perfectly what we need spiritually at any particular time. Many a teacher has had the experience of visiting an assembly with a word of teaching or admonition which they have discovered afterwards was perfectly suited to meet a present need in that assembly.

3. Expressions of Praise

The second reference to the believer's heart is contained in the phrase, "in psalms and hymns and spiritual songs, singing with grace in your hearts to the Lord" (Col 3.16). Paul instructs us how we are to use our voices. In Colossians 3.8, we are to put off filthy communication out of our mouths;

in chapter 4 verse 6 we are exhorted to let our "speech be alway with grace, seasoned with salt". However, we can do more than speak; we can also sing. This is the subject of our consideration. There are three basic questions to consider: To whom do we sing? What do we sing? How do we sing? The answers to these questions are addressed by the apostle.

To whom do we sing? Who is listening? Here we learn that we sing "to the Lord". Elsewhere, the Lord leads our praise - "in the midst of the church I will sing praise unto thee" (Heb 2.12) - but here the Lord is listening to the song of His saints, whether collectively or individually. What an amazing thought: our Lord is interested in the song of our hearts! While the sound of beautiful singing is indeed pleasant to our ears, the focus for the Lord is our hearts. More on this point shortly. Now, if we are singing to the Lord, it clearly follows that the subject matter of the singing is important. This leads us to the second of our questions: What do we sing? There is a threefold source of material to be sung: "psalms ... hymns ... spiritual songs". The connection with the preceding teaching should be clear: the Word of Christ is not only for teaching and admonishing, but it also provides the subject matter for song. There seems no reason to doubt that the word "psalms" refers to the Old Testament book bearing that name. This is an inspired collection of poems. There are, of course, other inspired songs in the Scriptures, such as the song of redemption (Exodus 15), and the 'Servant Songs' in Isaiah (for example, Isaiah 50). As readers will be well aware, the scope of subjects covered in the Psalms is huge, from direct prophecies regarding Christ, to the range of experiences of saints. The "hymns" focus on songs of praise, and allows for compositions which are not contained in the Scriptures but which are clearly based on the Scriptures. The "spiritual songs" are other compositions, again, not inspired, but containing spiritual content. Though many experiences of the saints of this age are found expressed in the Psalms, this is a unique age, with unique blessings. For example, we will not find the Rapture of the saints in the Psalms, but we can compose a spiritual song based on the revealed doctrine of New Testament Scriptures to express in song our hope of the soon return of the Lord to the air (1 Thess 4.13-18). Similarly, we might wish to express in song the truth of the Lord's Supper, which again is not found in the Psalms, but can also be composed as a spiritual song based on

New Testament revelation (for example, 1 Corinthians 11.23-34). Readers will be able to multiply other examples. The point is, in addition to the inspired Book of Psalms, we have considerable flexibility to sing hymns of praise and spiritual songs, so long as these compositions are in keeping with the Word of Christ. Since we are singing to the Lord, we will want to be sure that what we sing is true. Our hymns and spiritual songs should be accurate when measured against the Word of Christ. Why would any believer want to sing statements to the Lord which are not true?

The last matter is also of great moment. How do we sing? We sing "with grace in [our] hearts to the Lord" (Col 3.16). As Samuel learned, "the LORD looketh on the heart" (1 Sam 16.7). The same is true for the saints today. Our song arises from a sense of the grace of God in our hearts. This is our appreciation of the unmerited favour of God to us in Christ; all that we have spiritually is the result of God's grace, and this should promote expressions of praise. That the heart is involved implies that it is not merely the sound of our voices which is important. The exercise of the heart is vital. What does this mean? As noted previously, the heart is the seat of understanding (Ps 45.1; Lk 2.19), of faith (Prov 3.5; Rom 10.9-10), and of convictions (Dan 1.8; Acts 11.23). In this context, we should understand what we sing, we should believe what we sing, and we should have firm convictions about the subjects of our songs. Here, the focus is not so much on the musical sound that is made, but on the intelligence of the saint in so singing to the Lord, with appreciation for the grace of God.

4. The Activity of the Believer

The final two headings from the introduction are contained in the words of Colossians 3.17: "And whatsoever ye do in word or deed, do all in the name of the Lord Jesus, giving thanks to God and the Father by him". It is clear that this is a very broad statement about the words and work of the believer. Whatever we say and do is to be said and done in the Name of the Lord Jesus. This is a high standard indeed but, after all, in the new man, "Christ is all, and in all" (v 11). Speaking and doing in the Name of the Lord Jesus implies His absence. He is in Heaven, but involves us as His representatives here, where we speak and act as under His authority and for His glory. Were this truth to grip our hearts, it would revolutionise how we speak and act. With what care we would speak if all we said was in the Name of the Lord Jesus. All our words should be worthy of Him. When our Lord spoke, there was no wasted or flippant word; each word had weight. Again, with regard to our actions, what care we would take if all was to be done in the Name of the Lord Jesus. This principle should regulate all our activities.

While the terms of verse 17 are very broad, these words also need to be understood in the immediate context of verses 12-17. In particular, the teaching and admonishing of verse 16 must be given in the Name of the Lord Jesus; He is the ultimate authority for doctrine and practice. Again, the teaching and admonishing needs to be given in a Christ-like way, not only in terms of content, but in regard to the spirit and manner in which this ministry is performed. We recall that our Lord was "full of grace and truth" (Jn 1.14). Similarly, the actions enjoined on us in verses 12-13 require a Christ-like spirit in showing kindness, forbearance and forgiveness. When showing these Christ-like virtues we are to do it in the Name of the Lord Jesus. He is in Heaven, but His people are to act as His representatives here. Looking ahead from chapter 3 verse 18 to verse 1 of chapter 4, the actions required of the wife, the husband, the child, the father, the servant and the master all come within the scope of this principle, which brings a great dignity to living for Christ, and living out Christ, in the context of daily life.

5. The Giving of Thanks

This weighty section of practical exhortations concludes with a call to thanksgiving: "giving thanks to God and the Father by him" (Col 3.17). Reference to thanksgiving has already been found in Colossians 1.12, 2.7 and 3.15. In 1.12, the focus is upon one reason for giving thanks - on account of what the Father has done for us. In 2.7, the emphasis is on the degree of thanksgiving; in 3.15, the focus is on the fact that we should be thankful. In 3.17, the emphasis is on the Person to whom our thanksgiving is directed, and the Person in whose Name this thanksgiving is given. While we sing "to the Lord", we are to express thanksgiving to "God and the Father" by "him". Who is the "him"? It would seem to be the Lord. Thus, our offering of thanksgiving is mediated by the Lord to "God and the Father".

The reader is left to assemble the wide range of reasons and subjects for thanksgiving, which can be found as we make our way through this wonderful letter. May we take account of the two Godward spiritual exercises just discussed. We should sing to the Lord with appropriate conditions in our hearts, and give thanks to God the Father. These are exercises which we can fulfil both individually and collectively. The new man is not only marked by the virtues detailed in Colossians 3.12-14, but also by praise and thanksgiving.

Chapter 10

Personal Relationships (3.18 - 4.6)

Christian life is not lived in isolation. We need to interact with others, both believers and unbelievers. The manner of our conduct in these relationships is the subject of this section. We are to manifest Christ in our family and business relationships, as set forth in these Scriptures:

Wives, submit yourselves unto your own husbands, as it is fit in the Lord. Husbands, love your wives, and be not bitter against them. Children, obey your parents in all things: for this is well pleasing unto the Lord. Fathers, provoke not your children to anger, lest they be discouraged. Servants, obey in all things your masters according to the flesh; not with eyeservice, as menpleasers; but in singleness of heart, fearing God: and whatsoever ye do, do it heartily, as to the Lord, and not unto men; knowing that of the Lord ye shall receive the reward of the inheritance: for ye serve the Lord Christ. But he that doeth wrong shall receive for the wrong which he hath done: and there is no respect of persons. Masters, give unto your servants that which is just and equal; knowing that ye also have a Master in heaven. Continue in prayer, and watch in the same with thanksgiving; withal praying also for us, that God would open unto us a door of utterance, to speak the mystery of Christ, for which I am also in bonds: that I may make it manifest, as I ought to speak. Walk in wisdom toward them that are without, redeeming the time. Let your speech be alway with grace, seasoned with salt, that ye may know how ye ought to answer every man (Col 3.18 - 4.6).

The practical teaching of the apostle in chapter 3, up to this point, has been general in character; that is, it applies equally to all believers, no matter their gender, age or social status. Now, Paul gives specific instructions to various groups within the assembly at Colosse. This teaching can be divided into three: in 3.18-21, the teaching focuses on family relationships; in 3.22 - 4.1, the instruction deals with the conduct of both servants (slaves) and masters; in 4.2-6, the exhortations are more general, including dealings with unbelievers. We need to be clear that the practical teaching of the apostle concerning the new man does not simply apply to the character and conduct of believers in assembly gatherings, but it is to be seen in the home and workplace too. The effects of the Gospel on our lives are far-reaching and extensive. We must avoid the temptation of compartmentalising our lives.

Family Relationships (3.18-21)

Four groups are identified, namely, wives, husbands, children and fathers. While an individual needs to accept the specific instructions given, it is important to see that the four categories are grouped in two relationship-pairs: wives and husbands, children and fathers. We will comment further on this pairing later. The structure of the verses is straightforward to observe:

- *For the wife*, there is an instruction: "submit", and also a supporting reason: "as it is fit in the Lord" (3.18).
- *For the husband*, there is an instruction: "love your wives", and a further instruction: "be not bitter against them" (3.19).
- *For the children*, there is an instruction: "obey your parents in all things", and also a supporting reason: "for this is well pleasing unto the Lord" (3.20).
- *For the fathers*, there is an instruction: "provoke not your children to anger" and, again, a supporting reason: "lest they be discouraged" (3.21).

This simple analysis shows that the husbands are given two instructions; the other three categories are each given one. While being faithful in each of these relationships involves many aspects, Paul identifies one key instruction in three cases, and two for the husbands. In the parallel passage in Ephesians 5 and 6, the same relationships are discussed, and the same basic instructions given, with somewhat different supporting reasons. The responsibility of husbands is considered in some detail in Ephesians, with a parallel being drawn between the behaviour of the husband and Christ's love and activity in relation to the Church.

Turning our attention to verses 18-19, we find the instructions given to husbands and wives. This, of course, takes us back to the beginning (Gen 1.26-27; 2.21-25). At Colosse, there may well have been women who were not wives, but all the wives were women – they were female. Again, there may have been men who were not husbands, but the husbands were all men – they were male. This is the clear teaching of Scripture, no matter present-day perversions.

The wife is instructed to submit to her husband, who loves her and is not bitter towards her. The husband is instructed to love his wife, who submits to his headship. This is divine order. While each is responsible to the Lord for obeying these instructions, there can be no doubt that a wife will find it easier to submit to a husband who loves her and is not bitter towards her. In other words, the conduct of one certainly impacts the other. The basic idea in the word "submit" is to rank under.[32] It is primarily a military term, involving the acceptance of a higher authority. This must not be confused with any sense of inequality: in Christ, the husband and wife have equal standing; in the Lord, they have differing roles. Nor does the statement infer that the wife is any less spiritual, talented or knowledgeable than her husband, as the example of the wife in Proverbs 31.10-31 clearly demonstrates. The statement does, however, imply that, in marriage, the principle of headship holds, as is made clear in Ephesians 5.23: "For the husband is the head of the wife, even as Christ is the head of the church". This order is not a matter of negotiation between the couple concerned; it is the expression of the mind of God. By entering into the marriage relationship, the husband takes on a role of headship, and his wife assumes a role of subjection to her husband. The clause, "as it is fit in the Lord", means that the wife's subjection to her husband is her duty under the Lordship of Christ. Having accepted Jesus as Lord, she must now bow to His authority and accept it as her duty to the Lord to submit to her husband. It may be that her husband does not meet his obligations, but she still submits to him, as an act of obedience to the Lord. The following point must be clearly understood: it is not for a husband to put his wife in subjection to him; it is for him to love his wife. The instruction to the wife is to submit; to the husband, the instruction is to love.

The very fact that Scripture exhorts husbands to love their wives suggests that this is an all-too-common failing. For the husband who loves his wife, the wellbeing of his wife is his concern, whether this be physical, emotional or spiritual. He wants the best for her. His love is shown here in one particular aspect: he is not "bitter against her". He does not treat or speak to his wife harshly or sharply; he is patient and thoughtful of her needs, and avoids thoughtless nagging and fault-finding which crushes her spirit. This thoughtful, caring demonstration of love is what every Christian wife has a right to expect from her husband. The sacrificial nature of this love is made clear in the parallel passage in Ephesians 5.25: "Husbands, love your wives, even as Christ also loved the church, and gave himself for it". No greater sacrifice can be conceived; in giving Himself, Christ gave all for the Church. The plain and challenging teaching for husbands is that Christ's love and self-sacrifice is the pattern for husbands to follow. It is also what every Christian wife should rightly expect.

The second pair of relationships is that of children and fathers. While children are to obey their parents (both their father and mother), it is the responsibility of the fathers that is taken up by the apostle. The instruction for children is simple to state but, as many of us have discovered, not so easy to fulfil, especially, it seems, in teenage years. It is telling that we are shown the blessed example of the Lord Jesus (Lk 2.41-52) just as He entered this phase of His life on Earth. Luke notes, "he went down with them, and came to Nazareth, and was subject unto them" (v 51), even though "they understood not the saying which he spake unto them" (v 50). Why should a child obey their parents? The reason is also an encouragement to the child: it "is well pleasing unto the Lord". A believing child, having accepted Jesus as Lord, wants to please the Lord. They may ask themselves how they can be pleasing to the Lord in the sphere of the home. Here is one specific way open to them every day: by obeying their parents. This elevates everyday family life; for children there is the opportunity to be well pleasing to the Lord, simply by obeying their parents.

The other side of this relationship-pair has to do with the actions of a father. The instruction to fathers is in the form of a prohibition: "provoke not your children to anger". The words "to anger" are inserted, but they give the sense. The idea in the word "provoke" is to stir up,[33] to excite, not in a positive sense, but in an evil way. It is to irritate the child. How might a father do this? The following clause throws light on the matter. The reason for the prohibition is that the action of a father may lead to the child being "discouraged". The basic idea is to be without courage or spirit, to lose heart. Lightfoot[34] defines this as "to go about their task in a listless, moody, sullen frame of mind". Abbot[35] gives the following explanation: "a child frequently irritated by overseverity or injustice, to which, nevertheless, it must submit, acquires a spirit of sullen resignation, leading to despair". May those of us who are fathers avoid such provocation of our children that can cause a tragic state of despair.

Social Relationships: Servants and Masters (3.22 - 4.1)

Evidently, there was a wide social spectrum who had to live and work together as brethren and sisters in the assembly at Colosse. Paul's teaching in these verses was given to regulate the conduct of slaves who were believers, and masters who also were believers. In other words, these verses show the application of spiritual principles to those who found themselves in these roles. It is important to note that the Gospel did not overturn the prevailing social order of its day. While, thankfully, we do not have slaves and masters in the same way today, a possible application might be made to employees and employers. The teaching can be summarised thus: servants were to obey their earthly masters, and masters were to be just and equitable in dealing with their servants.

It is important to note the reference to the Godhead in these verses:

- "Fearing God" (3.22)
- "Ye serve the Lord Christ" (3.24)
- "Ye also have a Master in heaven" (4.1)

The thrust of Paul's argument was to elevate the daily, and perhaps menial, chores of the slave to the status of service to the Lord Christ while, at the same time, reminding the earthly master that he was, in fact, a slave to his heavenly Master. Thus, the behaviour of both would be regulated.

Verse 22 of chapter 3 shows that Paul was concerned about the obedience of believing slaves: they were to "obey in all things your masters according to the flesh". They were to fulfil their obligations to their master, even though this might not have been particularly appealing. We are not, of course, to see in the expression "all things" justification for wrongdoing, or activities which would mean disobeying God. Rather, in the general round of activities which a slave was duty-bound to fulfil, they were to obey. The manner of this obedience is developed both in a negative and a positive way. Negatively, their obedience was not to be "with eyeservice, as menpleasers". There are a number of ways to understand the term "eyeservice". It may, for example, describe the reluctant obedience that only renders superficial service – doing the items that can be seen by the master, and neglecting to carry out one's duties thoroughly. Alternatively (or, indeed, also), the expression could refer to that obedience which is carried out only when the master is present, and is neglected when he is absent. Either way, such service exemplifies the term "menpleasers". It is activity simply motivated to please men, including the possibility of pleasing men at the sacrifice of principle. The key point is that such service is not pleasing to God. The application to employees is clear – the believer is to be diligent and conscientious in fulfilling their responsibilities to their employer at all times.

Positively, the obedience of the slave is to be with "singleness of heart, fearing God". The idea is the undivided and wholehearted obedience of one who fears God, who looks beyond the natural circumstances, who obeys with the desire to please God, and certainly wishes to avoid displeasing Him. This is very helpful. A common problem for believers is not elevating the domestic and mundane to see the opportunity of pleasing God in these activities. After all, our Lord worked for years as a carpenter in Nazareth, at the end of which He received the commendation of His Father (Lk 3.22).

Verses 23 and 24 develop the thought that the daily activities of the slave were to be regarded as opportunities to serve Christ. Slaves were to look beyond their "masters according to the flesh" and see their heavenly Master, "the Lord Christ". The consequence was, "whatsoever ye do, do it heartily to the Lord, and not unto men". What a wonderful principle for daily living. In each activity, no matter how small, or seemingly unimportant, we are to carry it out with undivided attention, knowing that we are doing it for the Lord. This way of viewing our daily round of duties will help us to always do our best. Verse 24 explains the exhortation of verse 23. Why should we so serve? Paul advances two related reasons. Firstly, it is from the Lord that we will receive the reward of the inheritance and, secondly, we "serve the Lord Christ". Taking the latter first, Paul states a principle true of every believer – we "serve the Lord Christ". The mention of the "Lord" stresses His absolute authority over us and, by the same token, our complete submission to Him. The value of this verse, in the context, is to show that serving the Lord is not restricted to what we might regard as spiritual service alone; it includes the daily activities which make up much of our lives. Such service will receive from the Lord a reward - He will recompense. It may have been that a particular slave had an unjust master; the believing slave was to be encouraged to know that they would receive from the Lord a just payment for their toil. This repayment is described as "the inheritance", the future lot of the believer, including the place the believer will have in the coming Kingdom of the Lord Jesus. This section brings to our attention an aspect of the Judgment Seat of Christ which we tend to neglect. While the review of our spiritual service is a vital part, so too is how we have served the Lord as servants, or as employees, if we make this application.

Verse 25 contains a warning, made in the context of the duty of slaves to obey their masters. For the slave who does "wrong" there will be consequences now - he "shall receive for the wrong which he hath done" - along with the Lord's verdict in the future. The principle in operation is this: "there is no respect of persons". In the context, being a believing slave did not negate the duty of that slave to obey his master according to the flesh; rather, it gave greater cause for him to do so. The verse applies equally to masters.

There were some in the assembly who owned slaves; they had slaves in their household. How were they to treat these servants? Two instructions are given: they were to be "just" and "equal" (4.1), or equitable. They were not to exploit the position of authority they had over their servants as a pretext for unrighteous treatment of those individuals (whether or not they were believers), and they were to deal equitably with each one. They were to remember that they, too, were servants of a heavenly Master, the Lord Himself.

To sum up the teaching: the believing servant was to be the best of servants from the standpoint of the master; the believing master was to be the best of masters from the standpoint of the servant. The application to the employee and employer relationship should be clear but, to be explicit, the Christian employee should be the best of employees from the perspective of the employer, and the Christian employer should be the best of employers from the perspective of the employee. To be known as a Christian in the workplace, and not to do a good job, is a blot on the testimony. Likewise, employers who are known as Christians, yet are mean-minded and unjust, do much harm to the testimony of Christ.

There is a further application to be made here. While one might not be a master, or even an employer, many of us hold, or have held, positions of responsibility as managers or leaders in a business context. In such roles, we have authority over groups of our fellow-employees. The principles applying to masters also hold in this application. How are we viewed as managers? Are we regarded by those under us as just and equitable in our dealings? In the author's experience, what employees look for in a manager is fairness, consistency and compassion. To be a manager in the workplace, and known to be a Christian, places the same responsibilities before the Lord as those described as masters in the flesh here in the Epistle to the Colossians.

One final remark may be made about the teaching from 3.18 - 4.1. The principles applied in specific ways by the apostle are based on the foundation laid in 3.12-17. All believers are now "new", and new conduct and characteristics are to be seen, not only in the sphere of the assembly, and not only in family relationships, but also in the social setting. The change which is the result of salvation is to be seen in my dealings in all aspects of my life. We must avoid the error of compartmentalising our lives; Christ is to be seen in my assembly life, family life and business life. What a challenge this is!

Relationships with those who "are without" (4.2-6)

The practical ministry of the letter to the Colossians largely concludes in chapter 4 verses 2-6. Having given specific teaching to particular categories of individuals, Paul turns back to general instructions for the whole assembly. The instructions can be simply summarised:

- *Pray* – speaking to God (4.2-3)
- *Walk* – living before unbelievers (4.5)
- *Speak* – answering men (4.6)

The Colossians were themselves the subject of the prayers of Paul (1.9-11), and also of Epaphras (4.12-13). They did, however, need to pray themselves and for themselves. With this in mind, we find four instructions relative to their prayer life:

1. Continuance in Prayer
2. Vigilance in Prayer
3. Gratitude in Prayer
4. Specific Requests in Prayer

The first instruction is simply to continue to pray. This very act shows two things: firstly, that we continue to be needy and, secondly, that it is God alone who continues to be the One who can meet that need. The word 'continuance' carries the idea of persistence in, busying oneself in, devoting oneself to. This implies a positive discipline in one's life to the matter of prayer. It is viewed here as an integral part of the believer's life, requiring time to be dedicated to this spiritual exercise. As readers will know experientially, this is no trivial matter, and requires the determined development of a discipline in one's daily routine to devote time to prayer.

In the exercise of prayer, the believers had to be vigilant for the welfare of their fellow-saints - they were to be marked by watchfulness. What does this involve? Presumably, the Colossians would pray for one another on a regular basis. These prayers for each member of the assembly would be specific to the individual, taking account of how that believer was getting on. We may become aware of health issues in our fellow-saints, of family or employment issues, as well as spiritual problems, and these naturally become the subject matter of private prayers for those individuals. In this sense, we are watching out for our fellow-saints in prayer. There is also the thought of watching out for spiritual danger to our fellow-saints, and making this the subject of prayer. Spiritual believers will observe changes in the life and behaviour of their fellow-saints which may not be spiritually advantageous; this they should make the subject of prayer for those particular saints. Just as we are to be aware of changes in our body which may be signatures of a physical ailment, so we need to be similarly aware in the spiritual sphere. In the context of the assembly at Colosse, there was the pressing need for watchfulness in relation to Gnostic teachers and their influence on the thinking of the saints. We, too, need to be vigilant in this regard.

Vigilance in prayer is but one element of the prayer life of the believer. Gratitude is a second necessary element. There is so much for which to be thankful to God. The first chapter of this letter is largely an expression of thanksgiving from the apostle (1.3-8, 12-20, for example), and in chapter 2 verse 7 he anticipates the spiritual development of the believer to result in "abounding therein with thanksgiving". As the saint grows in their personal appreciation of "the faith" (1.23), this becomes the subject of thanksgiving. In chapter 4 verse 2, the thanksgiving is connected to watchfulness. As we watch for each other and pray accordingly, we look to see God's answers to our supplications, which become appropriate subjects of thanksgiving. A second aspect is this: we should look out for thankworthy traits in our fellow-saints for which to give thanks. Seeing the progress of fellow-believers, younger believers developing their gift and contributing to the assembly, and the recovery of others, are all suitable subjects for thanksgiving. There is one danger we must avoid: some believers have developed the unhealthy trait of feeding on the failure of their fellow-saints. This focus on failure does nothing for the individual concerned, and only raises barriers to harmonious relationships in the assembly.

Verses 3 and 4 deal with Paul's specific request for prayer from the Colossians. Given that he prayed for them, they would doubtless wish to pray for him. Paul was looking for God to open to him an opportunity (described here as "a door of utterance") to fulfil his ministry in relation to the mystery of Christ. He was looking for opportunities to speak. Paul recognised that his imprisonment was the direct result of this stewardship, but also that it was his responsibility to make known the truth revealed through him; he desired to "make it manifest". He was confident that God would open such a door. This confidence did not, however, exclude Paul's desire for the Colossians to pray specifically that it might be so. Of course, Paul was released for a season, and we are sure that he continued to make known the "mystery of Christ" as he desired to do. There is a simple lesson for us in this apostolic request: our prayers for our fellow-believers need to be specific.

The second instruction has to do with the conduct of the believer, particularly in relation to unbelievers, but perhaps also including believers not in the assembly at Colosse. There are two instructions given in verse 5:

1. "Walk in wisdom"
2. "Redeeming the time"

Wisdom is the practical knowledge of what to do or say in the experiences of life. This is clearly vital in our interactions with "them that are without". We want to conduct ourselves in a manner "worthy of the Lord" (1.10), as representing Him here both in our actions and our words. Awareness of opportunity also plays a role here. Paul urged the Colossians to "[redeem] the time". This has the sense of buying up opportunities as they present themselves to us. Putting this another way, we are to be mindful to take opportunities in testimony as they arise for us. This verse highlights one other important truth: those "that are without" are watching and taking note of our lives and conduct. Unbelievers, or even believers who do not gather with us, will be quick to note (and possibly point out) inconsistencies in our lives. A lack of wisdom on our part will be seized on by those who are hostile to Christ.

The final element of the apostle's teaching relates to the speech of the believer. This certainly relates to the previous instruction; if we are wise, we will be careful what and how we speak. Verse 6 tells us that our speech is to be marked by two features:

1. "Grace"
2. "Seasoned with salt"

In the first, we are following the pattern of our Lord Himself: "And all bare him witness, and wondered at the gracious words which proceeded out of his mouth" (Lk 4.22). That the Lord used gracious words did not lesson the truthfulness of what He taught, as the incident in Nazareth gives ample witness. It does imply, however, that in His words He brought the grace of God to men, and used fitting words for each occasion. The Lord knew how to speak "a word in season to him that is weary" (Isa 50.4). This is often the challenge for us; even when we know what we want to say, we can give the message in the wrong way. Our words need to be "with grace". Secondly, our speech is to be "seasoned with salt". This is evidently a figurative expression where we need to consider the properties of salt, particularly its capacity to preserve from corruption. Our speech is to have a preservative quality, and to be free from corruption. Paul made this point explicitly in Ephesians 4.29: "Let no corrupt communication proceed out of your mouth, but that which is good to the use of edifying, that it may minister grace unto the hearers". We are to consider the quality of our speech. Is it good? Is it edifying? Does it impart grace to the hearers? In Ephesians 5.4, we are prohibited from "foolish talking, nor jesting, which are not convenient: but rather giving of thanks". Our speech is one very clear way in which we can be different from the unbeliever. The purpose is that we might know "how" to answer every man (Col 4.6). The idea may be that the believer is challenged as to their faith in Christ, and the truth relative to Christ, as well as the functioning of a New Testament assembly. In response, we need to know how to answer these questions. This requires both knowledge and wisdom. One specific case in the context of the Colossian epistle was the interactions of the saints with false teachers, who denied both the truth of the Person and work of Christ. The Colossians needed to be sufficiently well-versed in the content of this letter, so as to "know how ... to answer" such men.

In summary, there is no doubt that the teaching of Paul's letter is both deep and complex in parts. In these verses, Paul reduces the essence of our responsibilities to three very simple statements: pray, walk and speak. May we have grace to embrace these simple, but vital, exhortations.

Chapter 11

Paul's Friends and Fellow-Servants (4.7-18)

In Colossians 1.23-29, the letter began with an account of the two-fold ministry of the Apostle Paul. It is fitting that the letter should conclude with an account of those who served with Paul. Although he had a unique ministry, this did not preclude him serving with other saints, whose fellowship and service he evidently appreciated. The following section identifies individuals who were associated with Paul in his imprisonment:

All my state shall Tychicus declare unto you, who is a beloved brother, and a faithful minister and fellowservant in the Lord: whom I have sent unto you for the same purpose, that he might know your estate, and comfort your hearts; with Onesimus, a faithful and beloved brother, who is one of you. They shall make known unto you all things which are done here. Aristarchus my fellowprisoner saluteth you, and Marcus, sister's son to Barnabas, (touching whom ye received commandments: if he come unto you, receive him); and Jesus, which is called Justus, who are of the circumcision. These only are my fellowworkers unto the kingdom of God, which have been a comfort unto me. Epaphras, who is one of you, a servant of Christ, saluteth you, always labouring fervently for you in prayers, that ye may stand perfect and complete in all the will of God. For I bear him record, that he hath a great zeal for you, and them that are in Laodicea, and them in Hierapolis. Luke, the beloved physician, and Demas, greet you. Salute the brethren which are in Laodicea, and Nymphas, and the church which is in his house. And when this epistle is read among you, cause that it be read also in the church of the Laodiceans; and that ye likewise read the epistle from Laodicea. And say to Archippus,

Take heed to the ministry which thou hast received in the Lord, that thou fulfil it. The salutation by the hand of me Paul. Remember my bonds. Grace be with you. Amen (Col 4.7-18).

Paul's Companions (4.7-14)

The epistle concludes with a touching section in which we learn about some of the men who were with Paul - his companions. The function is two-fold. In verses 7 to 9, Paul informs the Colossians that he is sending Tychicus and Onesimus, presumably carrying the letter, who will be able to tell them more of Paul's situation. Secondly, in verses 10 to 14, various named brethren send their greetings to the assembly at Colosse.

The stated purpose of the visit of Tychicus and Onesimus is three-fold. Firstly, Tychicus would let the Colossians know about Paul's state; secondly, Tychicus would get a first-hand view of the state of the Colossian saints; thirdly, jointly with Onesimus, they would report to the Colossians "all things which are done here" (v 9). An unstated purpose, which is nevertheless likely, is that these two brethren would personally deliver the letter from Paul. Indeed, their credentials and the purpose of their visit forms part of the letter itself. Paul evidently had a high estimation of the spiritual worth of Tychicus. In verse 7, he uses three terms in his commendation of this brother:

1. A "beloved brother"
2. A "faithful minister"
3. A "fellowservant in the Lord"

As a "beloved brother", we are in the sphere of the family of God. Paul and Tychicus were brothers in the Lord. Paul regarded him with affection, and terms him a "beloved" brother. This was the genuine expression of Paul's heart towards Tychicus. Secondly, he was a "faithful minister". In his own divinely-given service, Tychicus had proved himself to be faithful in his ministry. This is not now the affection of one brother to another, but the sober assessment of an apostle regarding the divine service of another. Paul reckoned him to have been faithful in the work the Lord had given him to perform. This is a trait well worth emulating; after all, ultimate reward from the Lord is for faithfulness (Mt 25.21). Thirdly, Tychicus was a "fellowservant in the Lord". Paul had a deep affinity with Tychicus, borne out of the experience of serving the Lord together. Although Paul was imprisoned and Tychicus evidently at liberty, Tychicus was with Paul, certainly not ashamed of Paul's chain, and is viewed as a fellow-bondservant under the authority of the Lord. Many readers may be able to relate to this personally. There are saints with whom we have developed strong ties through sharing in some aspect of the work of the Lord. We rightly regard them, as Paul regarded Tychicus, as fellow-servants in the Lord. It is important to note, before continuing, that Paul does not use these terms indiscriminately. Indeed, concerning Onesimus, Paul wrote that he was a "faithful and beloved brother" (Col 4.9).

In addition to the undoubtedly important task of delivering this letter to the Colossians, which he expected to be read in the hearing of the assembly (v 16), Paul had three other tasks in mind. Firstly, Tychicus was to declare to the Colossians Paul's "state" (v 7). In fact, the word "state" is in the plural, literally, Paul's 'states'. Why so? Tychicus would let them know about various aspects of Paul's welfare. Being close to Paul, he knew how he was physically, emotionally, spiritually, and so on. By the same token, Paul was relying on Tychicus to learn about the 'states' of the Colossians. Here, the plural takes account of the varying states of different believers. While one might say that a particular assembly is in a good state, this does not imply that it is so uniformly with each believer in the assembly. There was likely a range of states in the assembly. For example, we learn about Archippus (v 17), who is exhorted to fulfil his ministry. Epaphras had perhaps expressed concern to Paul regarding this brother and, doubtless, Paul would be anxious to know if his exhortation had stimulated Archippus in the desired way. Thirdly, he would "comfort your hearts" (v 8). Tychicus would bring a ministry of comfort to the hearts of the Colossian saints. This is a blessed ministry to have - to bring a ministry of encouragement - and its value cannot be overstated. It is easy to focus on failure; it is another matter entirely to build up and encourage the saints with a positive ministry of Christ! Paul shows confidence in Tychicus that he would bring this benefit to the saints. This also shows a commendable trait in the apostle; he had confidence in his fellow-servants to help the saints. He saw beyond his own ministry, and recognised that others had also been divinely fitted to bring "nourishment" to the body (2.19). Fourthly, together with Onesimus, Tychicus would let them know "all things which are done here" (4.9). This expression is broader than Paul's state, and possibly relates to how the work of God in general was progressing. The reference to Onesimus is important. This would tie the letter to the Colossians to the letter to Philemon. From that epistle, we learn a little of the past life of Onesimus, prior to his coming to Rome and his conversion under the influence of Paul. The Epistle to Philemon was then written to take account of the possible difficulty which might well have arisen when Onesimus returned.

Paul's Salutations (4.15-18)

The contents of these final verses of the epistle may be simply summarised:

- The Greeting from Aristarchus, Marcus and Justus (4.10-11)
- The Greeting from Epaphras (4.12-13)
- The Greeting from Luke and Demas (4.14)
- The Greeting to the Brethren in Laodicea (4.15-17)
- The Final Greeting from Paul (4.18)

The Greeting from Aristarchus, Marcus and Justus (4.10-11)

From verse 10 to verse 14, Paul passes on the greetings of various named brethren to the saints at Colosse. There are three salutations in verses 10, 12 and 14. The first is from Aristarchus, Marcus (Mark) and Justus, the second from Epaphras, the third from Luke and Demas. Aristarchus, a man of Macedonia (Acts 19.29), was evidently imprisoned with Paul and is afforded the description "my fellowprisoner" (Col 4.10). One can only conjecture about the physical and emotional hardships they endured together; not surprisingly, therefore, Paul speaks of him in appreciative tones. Saints who have walked the path of hardship together value having a 'fellow' in the same circumstance. The time would arrive when Paul would not even have this; in 2 Timothy 4.16, he comments that "all … forsook me", yet, of course, he had the presence of the Lord: "Notwithstanding, the Lord stood with me, and strengthened me" (v 17). Aristarchus was not merely with Paul in the prison, but shared Paul's interests in the Colossian saints, so he also sends greetings to them.

The second named man who sends greetings to the Colossians is Mark, the nephew of Barnabas. It seems that the Colossians had already received a word about Mark, and should he come to Colosse they were to receive him. This suggests that, although he was at the time with Paul, he was at liberty, and there was the possibility that he might travel to Colosse. It is interesting that Paul did not send Mark with Tychicus and Onesimus, given the interest Mark had in visiting Colosse. It is well known that Mark had been taken with Paul and Barnabas on their first missionary journey (Acts 13.5), and that he had departed from them, returning to Jerusalem. Paul "thought not good" to take Mark on a return journey, resulting in a rift between Paul and Barnabas (15.38). That Mark was now with Paul says much for both men. Paul saw the value of Mark and his ministry (2 Tim 4.11), and that he had progressed from the personal failure of leaving the work at Pamphylia. Similarly, Mark did not hold it against Paul that he resisted taking him on his second missionary journey. Some comments on this incident seem appropriate. Failure and breakdown in service should not be ignored, as if they had not happened. For Paul, there had been a breach of trust; could he depend on Mark if he and Barnabas took him on their return journey? At the time, Paul evidently felt he could not. This does not imply that Paul had 'written-off' Mark for the future. It simply meant that Mark needed to prove himself. The same principle still holds: if we fail then we have let ourselves, the Lord and our fellow-saints down. The Lord restores, yet we need to regain the confidence of our fellow-servants and the saints more generally. We need to prove ourselves as reliable servants of the Lord.

The third named man is one Jesus, called Justus. Though little is known of this brother, he was a Jew and a fellow-worker with the apostle who, along with Mark, was a comfort to Paul. The expression, "these only are my fellowworkers unto the kingdom of God" (Col 4.11) seems strange, given the subsequent mention of Epaphras and Luke, for example. One possible explanation for this rather restricted statement, which seems to exclude the likes of Epaphras and Luke, is that it is qualified by the statement, "who are of the circumcision" (v 11). That is, Paul is thinking in a restricted sense. Of those of the circumcision, only Mark and Justus were his fellow-workers unto the Kingdom of God. The word 'workers' carries the thought of working with, being a helper or companion in the work. Paul valued the encouragement they gave him: they "have been a comfort unto me" (v 11). They lifted and cheered the heart of the apostle in difficult and trying circumstances. In application, may we be those who bring a similar encouragement to the Lord's dear people, many of whom are struggling to continue in difficult conditions. It is relatively easy to focus on the failure of the saints in ministry (usually dressed up as 'practical ministry'); it is another matter to bring a ministry to the saints which actually meets the need, which encourages, which gives the saints heart to go on! Mark and Justus were men who so comforted the apostle.

The Greeting from Epaphras (4.12-13)

We learned of Epaphras' role in chapter 1 verse 7 and, here, at the end of the letter, though absent from the Colossians, his interest in the assembly was clearly undiminished. Paul observes that he "is one of you" (4.12). This does more than imply that he came from Colosse; though he was absent from them, he was still of them, and they remained his chief concern. He still regarded himself as being one of the Colossian saints. His service was as a bondservant of Christ. He owned Christ as his Master, and his efforts and burden were for those who belonged to Christ in Colosse. Epaphras greeted the Colossians as one of them, who had faithfully preached to them the Gospel, and seen the assembly established. Though absent, his labour for them continued: "always labouring fervently for you in prayers" (v 12). This remarkable statement stresses the ongoing burden Epaphras had for the Colossian assembly. The "always" stresses the constancy of his exercise, "labouring" shows that his prayer life led to physical weariness, and "fervently" conveys the zeal and earnest concern evident to Paul as he witnessed, and perhaps listened to, the prayers of Epaphras. Epaphras had a well-defined goal in his prayers: he desired that the saints might "stand perfect and complete in all the will of God" (v 12). The idea in the word "perfect" is that of being full grown and mature; "complete" is the idea of full assurance or that which has reached full measure. This maturity and assurance would see them withstand the spiritual dangers which we have considered in chapter 2, and grow individually to be more like Christ, as we have noted in chapter 3. The "will of God" here includes all that God wills for His people, which in no way differs from what we have learned already in the epistle.

There are number of notable lessons for each of us. The first is simple, but vital: the labour of prayer is not to be regarded as a secondary service for the saints. As many will doubtless testify, we have known the value of the prayers of saints for us. Perhaps some readers feel that there are avenues of service which they are no longer able physically to pursue, but here is a valuable, nay vital, service for us all – to pray for the saints! A second lesson is that engaging in such prayer is not easy; here it is regarded as a labour, involving toil to the point of weariness. There was a physical cost for Epaphras, and for all who follow his example. Thirdly, Epaphras was ambitious for the saints. He knew the dangers they faced, yet had the highest thoughts for the progress of these believers. So, too, should we.

The time Epaphras had been with Paul convinced the apostle that he "hath a great zeal for you, and them that are in Laodicea, and them in Hierapolis" (4.13). He had a big heart for the saints in these locations; it would seem he had ministered to them, and they now held a special place in his heart. This was not simply a sentimental feeling, but a deep spiritual exercise for the preservation and progress of these believers. The Colossians knew this was a man who cared for them. Paul is letting them know in this letter that this was still the case, even though he was physically absent. Here is a great lesson for every servant who would minister the Word to the saints: the saints need to know we care for them; that we are not simply delivering a message, though this is vitally important, but that there is a genuine interest in them for their preservation and progress. This means we must not be aloof or unapproachable, but should be willing to take the time to get to know individual believers and their circumstances.

The Greeting from Luke and Demas (4.14)

Luke and Demas were evidently with Paul at this time. Of course, Luke would remain with Paul, whereas Demas would eventually depart (2 Tim 4.10) during Paul's second period of imprisonment. Paul's description of Luke is of interest: the "beloved physician" (Col 4.14). Here, Luke is referred to by his secular calling; no doubt his skills in this area may have proved beneficial to Paul and the wider company of disciples. However, he was of greater value in spiritual things, and would remain loyal to Paul to the end of the apostle's life (2 Tim 4.11).

The Greeting to the Brethren in Laodicea (4.15-17)

In Colossians 4.15-16, Paul requests the Colossian saints to pass on his greetings to the assembly at Laodicea, and to Nymphas, along with the assembly which met in his house, in particular. This accompanies the apostolic instruction for the Colossian letter to be read at Laodicea and, likewise, for the Colossians to hear the letter from Laodicea. These simple requests illustrate some important points. Firstly, the exchange of greetings is an expression of fellowship and mutual concern. That the Colossians would pass on Paul's greetings to the Laodiceans shows that there was communication and fellowship between these two autonomous assemblies. We still benefit and value such fellowship today. Secondly, the letter to the Colossians was of wider interest. While it was written to the Colossians, with the specific dangers they faced in mind, it was intended also to be of wider benefit. Likewise, the Colossians would profit from hearing the letter to Laodicea. Similarly, we still benefit today from the ministry Paul wrote to Colosse.

Verse 17 contains a personal exhortation to Archippus, who was one of the brethren in the assembly at Colosse. Perhaps Epaphras had spoken to Paul of his concern for this brother, and now Paul adds a brief word of exhortation as he closes the letter. One can only guess the reaction of Archippus when he heard his name included in this letter from the Apostle Paul, and the accompanying exhortation. Doubtless, Tychicus would report back, in due course, on the impact of these words. The exhortation is practical and weighty: "Take heed to the ministry which thou hast received in the Lord, that thou fulfil it" (v 17). The first key point is that Archippus had received his ministry from the Lord Himself. He was therefore responsible to the Lord for the extent to, and the manner in which, he fulfilled it. We all find ourselves in this position. Although our ministry is for the benefit of others, it is given to us by the Lord, and we are ultimately accountable to Him. In this light, Paul urges Archippus to "take heed to the ministry". This carries the idea of looking to his ministry, of intent and earnest contemplation with a view to completing it. Paul is concerned that, for whatever reason, Archippus' ministry might remain unfulfilled. This is a serious matter, and one with practical implications for every servant of the Lord. There are many reasons why we might not fulfil our ministry, but this Scripture amply stresses that we need to make fulfilling our divinely-given ministry our focus and priority.

The Final Greeting from Paul (4.18)

The epistle concludes with greetings from the apostle to the Colossians: "the salutation by the hand of me Paul" (v 18). Although they had never seen him, this personal greeting, along with the rich ministry of the letter, would show the personal interest Paul had in their spiritual preservation and growth. Although another may have written the letter, Paul personally signed it with his own hand. This both authenticated the apostle as the author and showed his personal interest. The saints need to know the servant cares! In reciprocal manner, Paul requested that they "remember my bonds" (v 18). He valued the interest of the saints in him, and appreciated their remembrance of him in his imprisonment.

The final words of the letter are touchingly simple: "Grace be with you. Amen" (v 18). The Colossians had come to know the grace of God in truth through their acceptance of the Gospel message (1.6), but grace was required in every step of the pathway. The letter began with a salutation of grace: "Grace be unto you, and peace, from God our Father and the Lord Jesus Christ" (v 2). The divine supply of grace from our Father and from our Lord is assured. Fittingly, Paul concludes with an expression of his desire that God's sufficient grace might remain with them. We most certainly need the same ourselves, both individually and collectively. The final word is "Amen". It is well known that the term means 'so let it be'. It was the heartfelt desire of the apostle regarding all he had written to the Colossians. As we weigh the rich yet practical teaching of this letter, may we all echo the same desire, "Amen".

Chapter 12

Postscript: Gnostic Error after Colossians

We are now left with a question: What happened to the dangerous Gnostic teaching after Paul had written Colossians? We have to fast-forward 30 or so years to when the Holy Spirit took up the Apostle John to write his epistles and Gospel. In the Colossian letter, it seems that, although the danger was a present one (Col 2.8), false teachers had not yet infiltrated the assembly, and Paul was able to give a general commendation (v 5). By the time John wrote, the situation had moved on. In his first epistle, he writes of those who "went out from us, but they were not of us; for had they been of us, they would no doubt have continued with us" (1 Jn 2.19). John highlights three elements of the error held by such. They denied "that Jesus is the Christ" (v 22), they denied "the Father and the Son" (v 22), and they "confess[ed] not that Jesus Christ is come in the flesh" (4.3; 2 Jn 7). Such were identified by John as "antichrists" (1 Jn 2.18, 22) and "liar[s]" (v 22). These individuals were against Christ, holding and propagating falsehoods about Him.

The denial that "Jesus is the Christ" (v 22) involved the assertion that the man Jesus was not the Christ; that the Spirit of Christ came upon Him at His baptism and left before the cross, so that it was Jesus, not Christ, who died. John specifically refuted this in his Gospel, when he wrote:

And many other signs truly did Jesus in the presence of his disciples, which are not written in this book: but these are written, that ye might believe that Jesus is the Christ, the Son of God; and that believing ye might have life through his name (Jn 20.30-31).

The denial of "the Father and the Son" (1 Jn 2.22) involved the rejection of the revealed nature of the Godhead as a tri-unity of co-equal, co-substantial and co-eternal Persons. The Gnostic envisaged a solitary supreme God, and rejected the Biblical revelation of the distinct Persons of the Godhead - Father, Son and Holy Spirit. We are still faced with sects who propagate the same disastrous error today. The reader of the Gospel of John will be well aware of the stress on the Father and the Son, and the distinctive ministry of the Holy Spirit.

The third element of denial was that "Jesus Christ is come in the flesh". The Gnostic regarded the physical universe as completely incompatible with God, and regarded flesh as intrinsically evil. The thought that God would be manifest in flesh was rejected. It is seldom appreciated that John deals extensively with this matter in his Gospel. We often regard the Gospel of John as the Gospel of the Son of God, hence dealing with the deity of Christ. While this is undoubtedly true, it is not the whole truth. John, as we will now outline, deals extensively with the humanity of Christ, with the crucial introductory statement, "the Word became flesh, and dwelt among us (and we beheld his glory, the glory as of the only begotten of the Father), full of grace and truth" (Jn 1.14). Indeed, the name "Jesus", which we rightly associate with the humanity of Christ (the name given at His birth, Lk 1.31, Mt 1.21, 25), occurs more often in John's Gospel than the Synoptic Gospels (245 references in John, 170 in Matthew, 93 in Mark and 97 in Luke). John records the historical witness of individuals (and the Lord Himself) to the fact that the Lord was a true Man. These references make a profitable study, which we will outline here.

In John 1.30, having declared publicly that the Lord was the "Lamb of God" (v 29), John the Baptist declared, "This is he of whom I said, After me cometh a man which is preferred before me: for he was before me". John was clear; the One who would come after him was "a man". Yet, this man was completely different to John in this respect: "he was before me". Although the Lord was born after John (Lk 1.56-57), He was before John, referring to His eternal, unoriginated existence (Jn 1.1). Hence, the Spirit of God connects the truth of the humanity of Christ with the eternality of His Being. On this account, John recognised that the Lord was "preferred" before Him; He merited far greater honour than John the Baptist could ever contemplate.

The second reference is found during the Lord's visit to Samaria (Jn 4). The unnamed Samaritan woman recognised that the Stranger with whom she spoke was a Jew (v 9). Furthermore, when she returned to the city, she announced, "Come, see a man, which told me all things that ever I did: is not this the Christ" (v 29). Again, there is indisputable testimony to the humanity of Christ, coupled here with His omniscience – He knew all about the woman, her past and present. She was convinced that He was the Christ (and He still is). By the end of the Lord's two-day stay in Samaria, many more held the same conviction, "that this is indeed the Christ, the Saviour of the world" (v 42).

During the last day of the Feast of Tabernacles, the officers sent to take the Lord returned empty-handed, but gave this telling testimony: "Never man spake like this man" (7.46), hence recognising that he was indeed a man, but that His words were unique. The following day, in a lengthy dialogue with the Jews, the Lord Himself declared, "But now ye seek to kill me, a man that hath told you the truth, which I have heard of God" (8.40). The Lord asserted His own humanity, and the truthfulness of the words He spoke, the source of these words being God Himself.

The testimony of the man who had been born blind (Jn 9) contributes to this theme. When he was interrogated by the neighbours as to how he now had sight, he witnessed, "A man that is called Jesus made clay, and anointed mine eyes, and said unto me, Go to the pool of Siloam, and wash: and I went and washed, and I received sight" (v 11). This wonderfully clear testimony recognised the humanity of the One who had healed him. The humanity and omnipotence of the Lord Jesus were undeniably coupled together.

Later, the Jews, in their opposition to Christ, justified their taking up stones to stone Him, "because that thou, being a man, makest thyself God" (10.33). They were absolutely clear that He was a man; they rejected that He was God. Of course, the truth is that He was always

God, yet had become a man. Finally, there was the notable declaration of Pilate (19.5): "Behold the man!". Pilate and the baying multitude were in no doubt as to the humanity of Christ – yet they failed to grasp that He was God manifest in flesh.

An additional line of evidence is provided by the Apostle John. He makes reference to the Lord's body (2.18-22; 19.38-42; 20.20, 27-28), the Lord's soul (12.27), and the Lord's spirit (11.33; 13.21). Man is a tripartite being, consisting of spirit, soul and body (1 Thess 5.23), and the incarnate Word is seen to have a body, soul and spirit, reinforcing that the Word had become flesh.

The abiding truth is that the Evil One will ensure that the pure doctrine of Christ is challenged in every generation. It is no different today. May the Spirit of God enable us to hold fast to the truth regarding the Person and work of Christ, along with the unique relationship which the Church, the Body of Christ, has with Him.

References

[1] F Rienecker & C Rogers, *Linguistic Key to the Greek New Testament*, pp 564-585.

[2] W E Vine, *Expository Dictionary of Bible Words*.

[3] Rienecker & Rogers, *Linguistic Key*, pp 564-585.

[4] Rienecker & Rogers, *Linguistic Key*, pp 564-585.

[5] T Bentley, *Colossians – What the Bible Teaches*.

[6] A Kenny, *A New History of Western Philosophy*, pp 55, 232.

[7] Kenny, *A New History*, pp 55, 232.

[8] Rienecker & Rogers, *Linguistic Key*, pp 564-585.

[9] A de Ville, *A Study of the Resurrection of Jesus Christ*, pp 122-123.

[10] Bentley, *Colossians*.

[11] Vine, *Expository Dictionary*.

[12] Vine, *Expository Dictionary*.

[13] A Neander, *General History of the Christian Religion and Church - Volume 2*.

[14] Vine, *Expository Dictionary*.

[15] Kenny, *A New History*, pp 55, 232.

[16] Vine, *Expository Dictionary*.

[17] Rienecker & Rogers, *Linguistic Key*, p 574.

[18] Rienecker & Rogers, *Linguistic Key*, p 576.

[19] Rienecker & Rogers, *Linguistic Key*, p 578.

[20] Rienecker & Rogers, *Linguistic Key*, p 578.

[21] Vine, *Expository Dictionary*.

[22] Rienecker & Rogers, *Linguistic Key*, p 578.

[23] Rienecker & Rogers, *Linguistic Key*, p 578.

[24] Rienecker & Rogers, *Linguistic Key*, p 579.

[25] Rienecker & Rogers, *Linguistic Key*, p 579.

[26] Rienecker & Rogers, *Linguistic Key*, p 579.

[27] Vine, *Expository Dictionary*.

[28] Rienecker & Rogers, *Linguistic Key*, p 579.

[29] Vine, *Expository Dictionary*.

[30] Vine, *Expository Dictionary*.

[31] Vine, *Expository Dictionary*.

[32] Vine, *Expository Dictionary*.

[33] Rienecker & Rogers, *Linguistic Key*, p 582.

[34] Rienecker & Rogers, *Linguistic Key*, p 582.

[35] Rienecker & Rogers, *Linguistic Key*, p 582.